Impressions of Alaska 2007

From Portage to Talkeetna and Beyond

By Roland Berg

ISBN 978-0-6151-4543-3

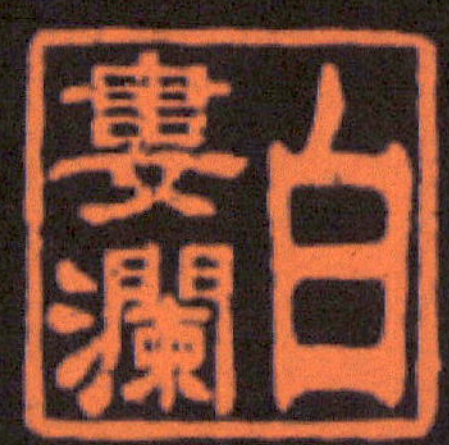

Published by

Digital Impressions Publishing

San Antonio, Texas U.S.A.

www.rolandberg.com

For my mother, Lillian Berg (1918-2001),
and my brother, Gary Wolinski (1944-2006),
they were my inspiration and my strength.

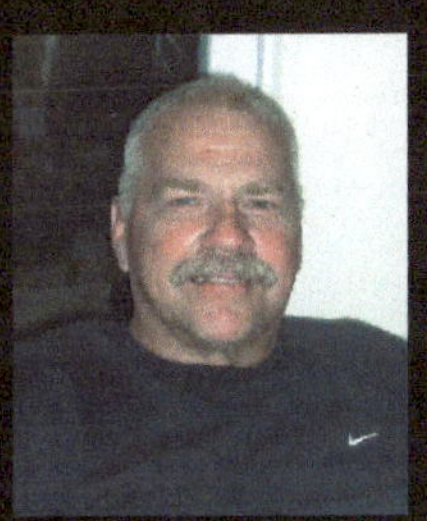
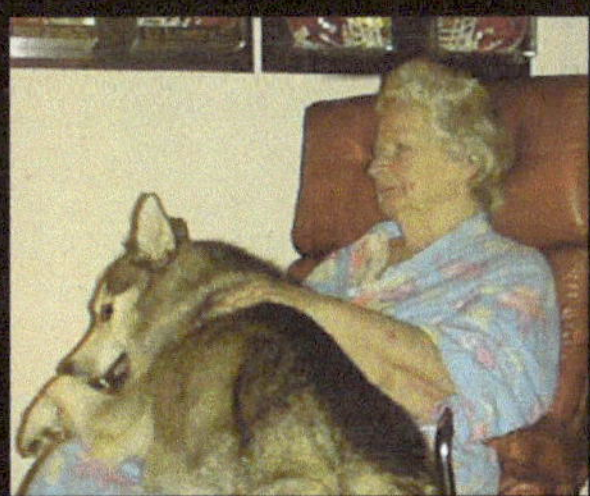

I wish that I could have shared
this experience with them.

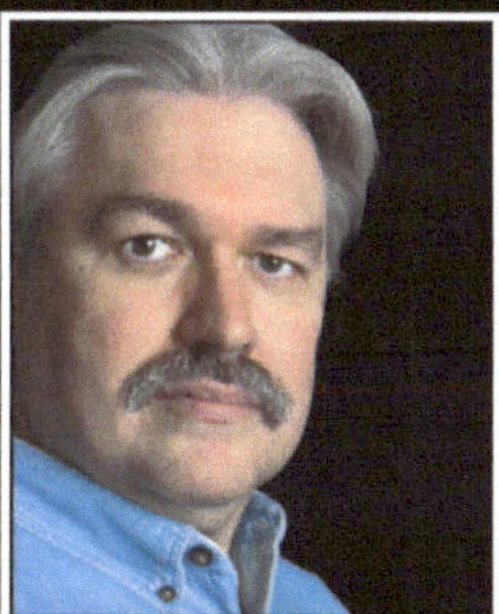

Artist's Statement

My earliest formal education in photography came at age 16. It was a summer program run by the CEPA Gallery in Buffalo, NY. It was sponsored by the Polaroid Corporation, and taught by Peter Layton. While I may not have understood them at the time, Peter taught me several lessons that have served me well over the years. He taught me early on to be disciplined and ensure that each image was fine-tuned in the darkroom to reach its full potential. The true importance of this discipline, and the meaning of his discussions of the emotion and feeling involved in the creation of images, have come vividly to the front of my mind as I have matured and transitioned my thought processes from that of taking pictures to that of creating art.

Later, I was fortunate enough to work for James Cavanaugh, an accomplished photographer, who became a mentor and friend through the early years. He taught me the importance of technical mastery of the craft of photography and helped expose me to others that would help me learn how to see, feel and create the images that I produce today.

Most recently, and perhaps most important to the development of my artistic thought, I have had the friendship of an artist whose work is widely recognized although he prefers to remain quietly and anonymously in the shadows. Through my relationship with him I have been exposed to both his art and his philosophy and this exposure has helped me grow artistically, professionally and personally and this has allowed me to see and experience the world through different eyes.

Today I work primarily in digital media, although I occasionally work in traditional formats as well. Images are personally created and hand edited to ensure that every detail supports the artistic intent of the image. Each image produced is the culmination of an average of 15-20 hours of pre- and post-production work.

My goal is to create images that are both aesthetically captivating and thought provoking. I strive to create images that will evoke a deep emotional response from everyone that encounters them. There is a story in each image that I create; a story that may have existed in the reality of a moment in time, the fantasy of my imagination, or my vision of the past or future. It may even be a story of your very own.

Thank you for allowing me to share my art with you.

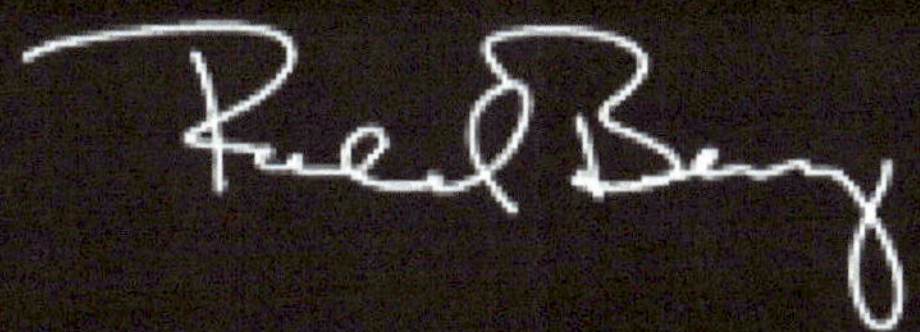

For more information visit www.rolandberg.com

Impressions of Alaska 2007

Table of Contents

The Alaskan countryside around Anchorage offers something for everyone. Nowhere else can a short drive expose you to scenes that are so dramatic and visually stimulating.

The drive down the Seward Highway winds along the coastal waters of the Cook Inlet. Look to one side and you see that the road is not far above sea level. Look to the other and see dramatic shear rock faces and mountains that rise thousands of feet. This contrast can be overwhelming at times as each turn reveals a new scene often more magnificent than the one you just left.

As you drive your emotions change from wonder and awe, as you are overcome by the surreal beauty of areas like Portage Lake, to a sense of sadness and reflection as you look at properties devastated by the earthquake of 1964; still standing as monuments to the disaster some 43 years later.

The Glenn Highway takes you to wonderful places like Thunderbird Falls, Eklutna Lake and eventually to communities like Palmer and Sutton while the Park Highway takes you to Wasillla, Willow and Talkeetna and eventually to Denali and Fairbanks.

The images that follow represent but a few moments in time that this wonderful land shared with me; that I now share with you. The images were captured using a variety of techniques including infrared and high dynamic range photography as well as more traditional methods.

I hope that the images will convey a sense of the majesty of this wonderful place to you.

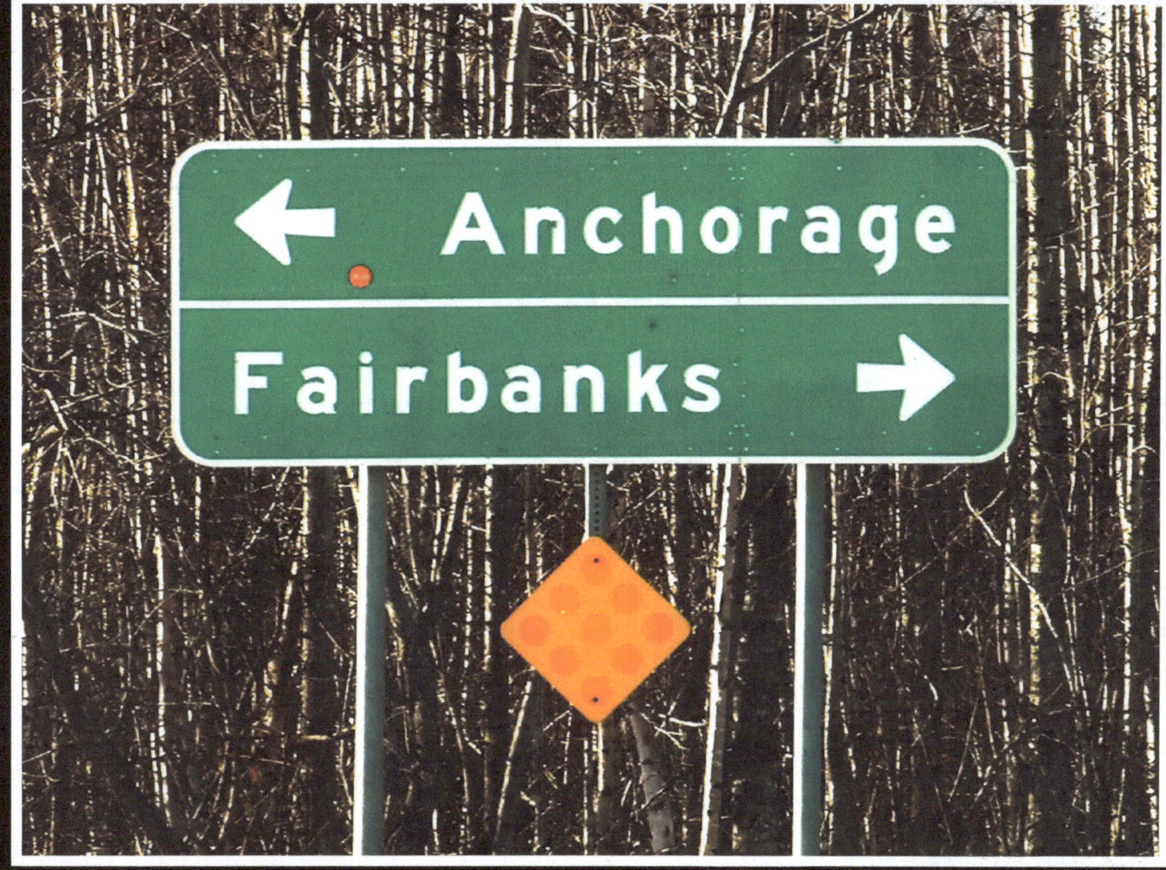
Anchorage
Fairbanks

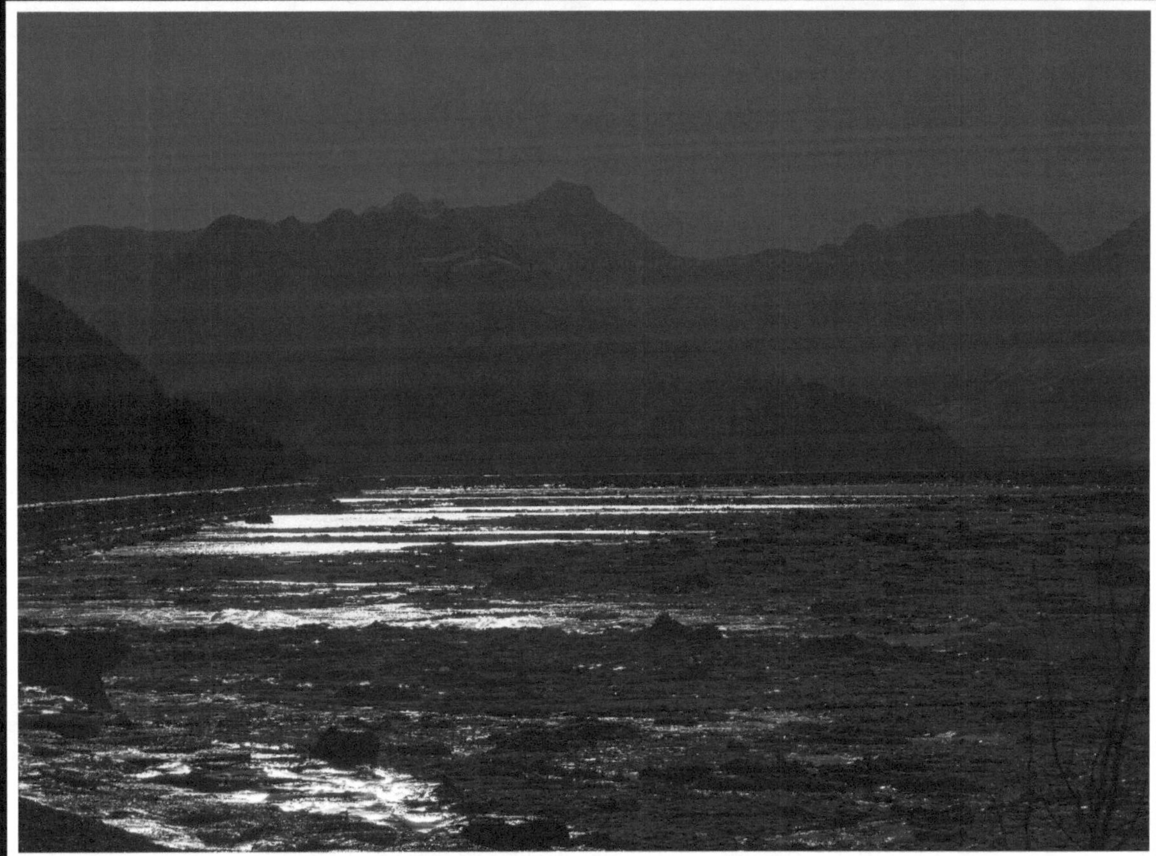

Impressions of Alaska 2007

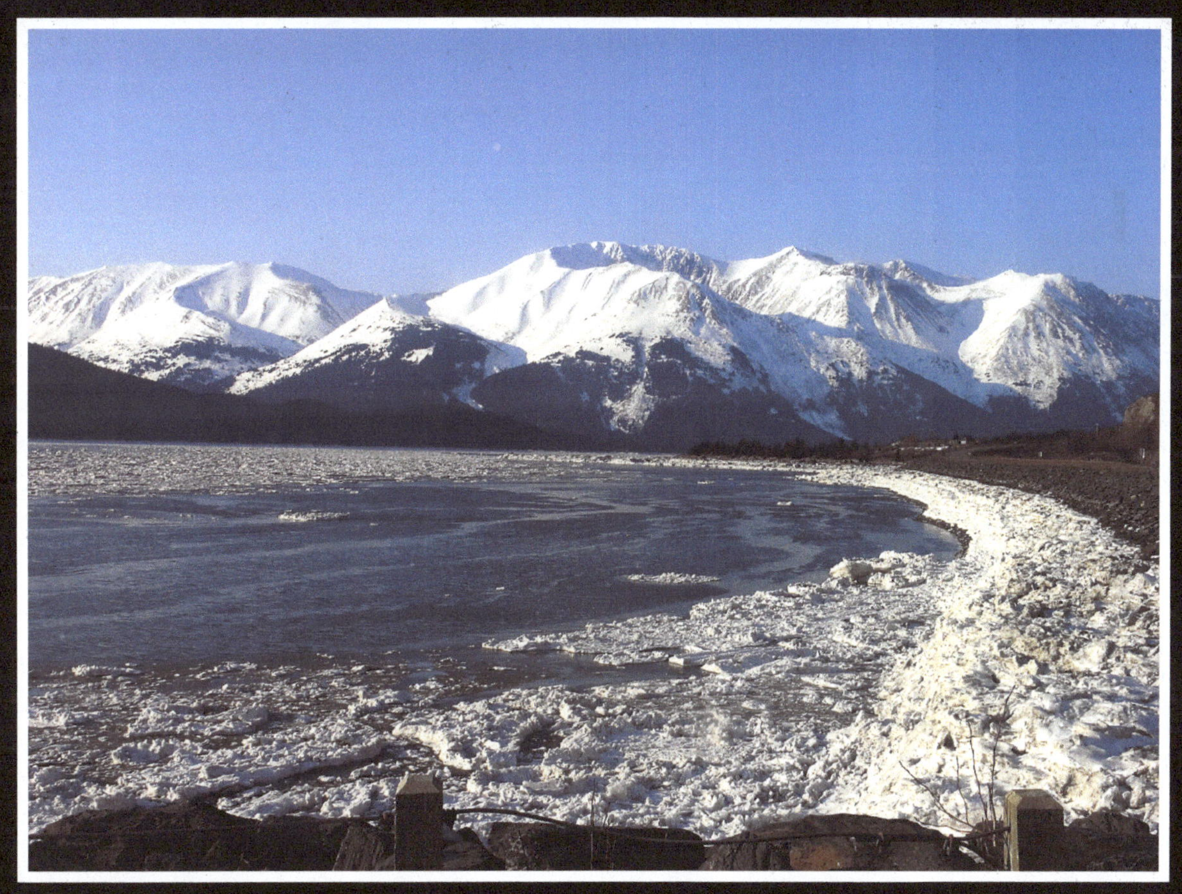

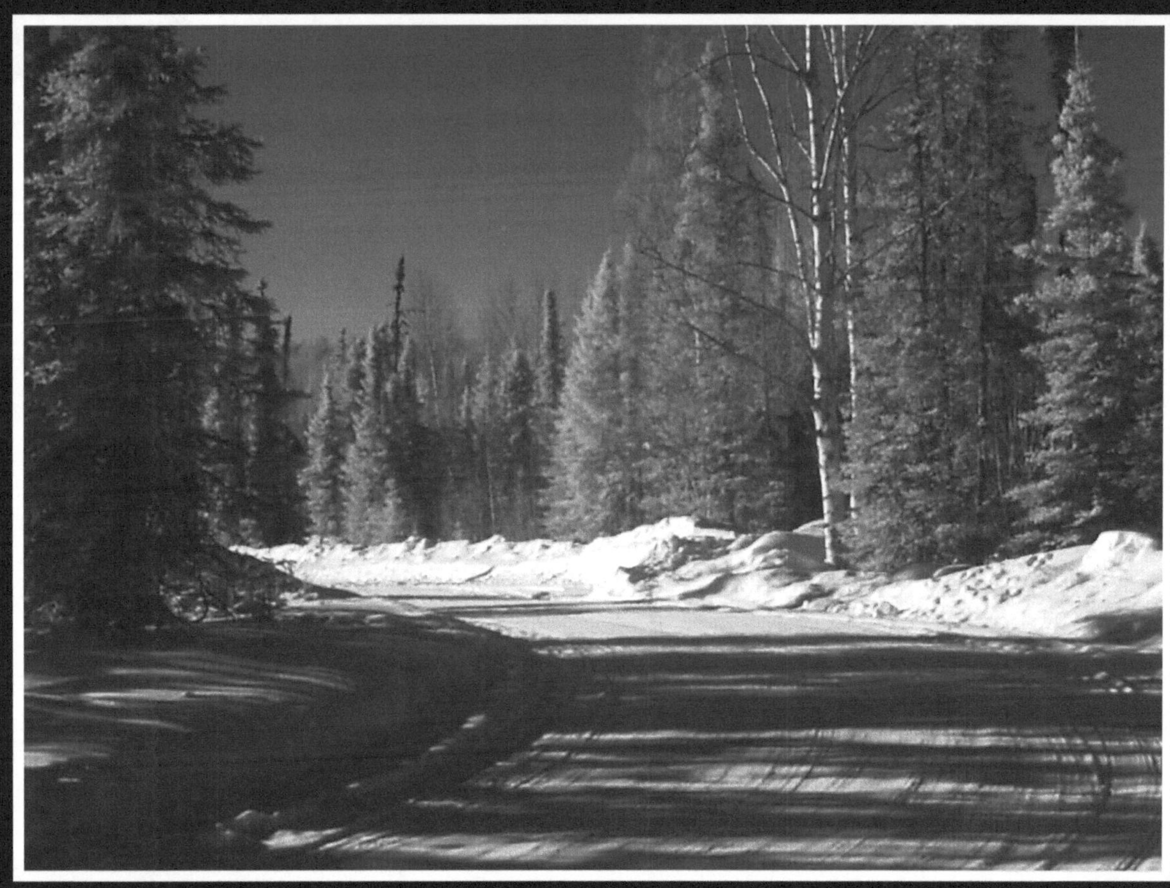

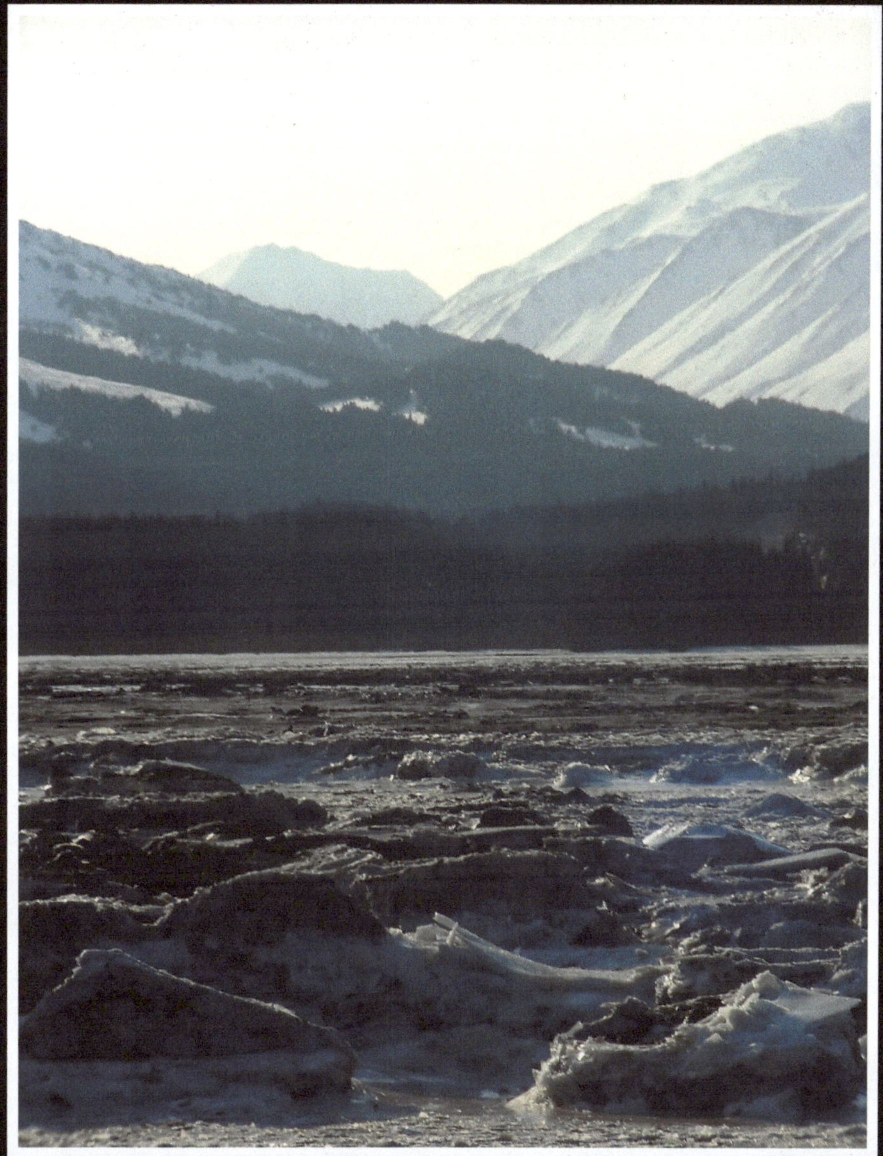

Earthquake Reminders I and II

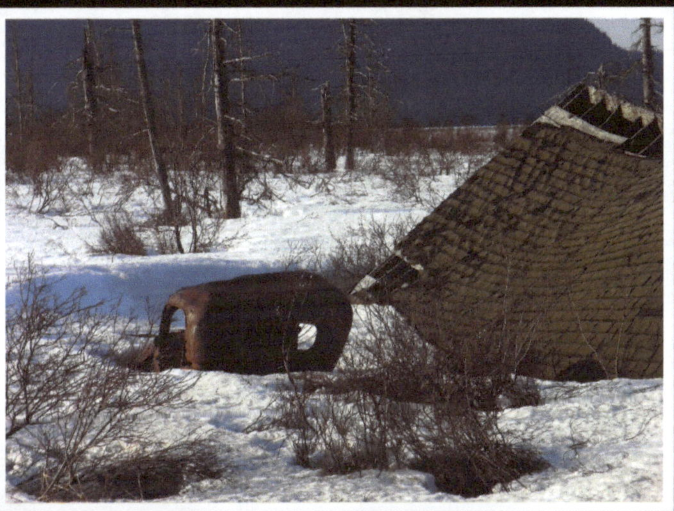

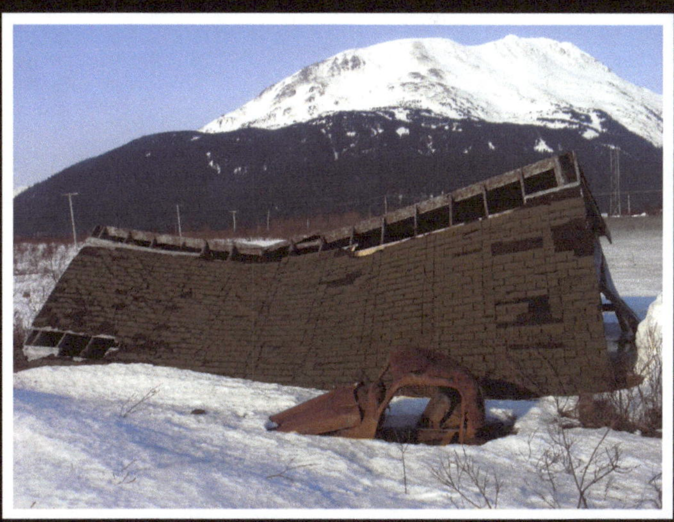

Impressions of Alaska 2007

Chugiak City Park II

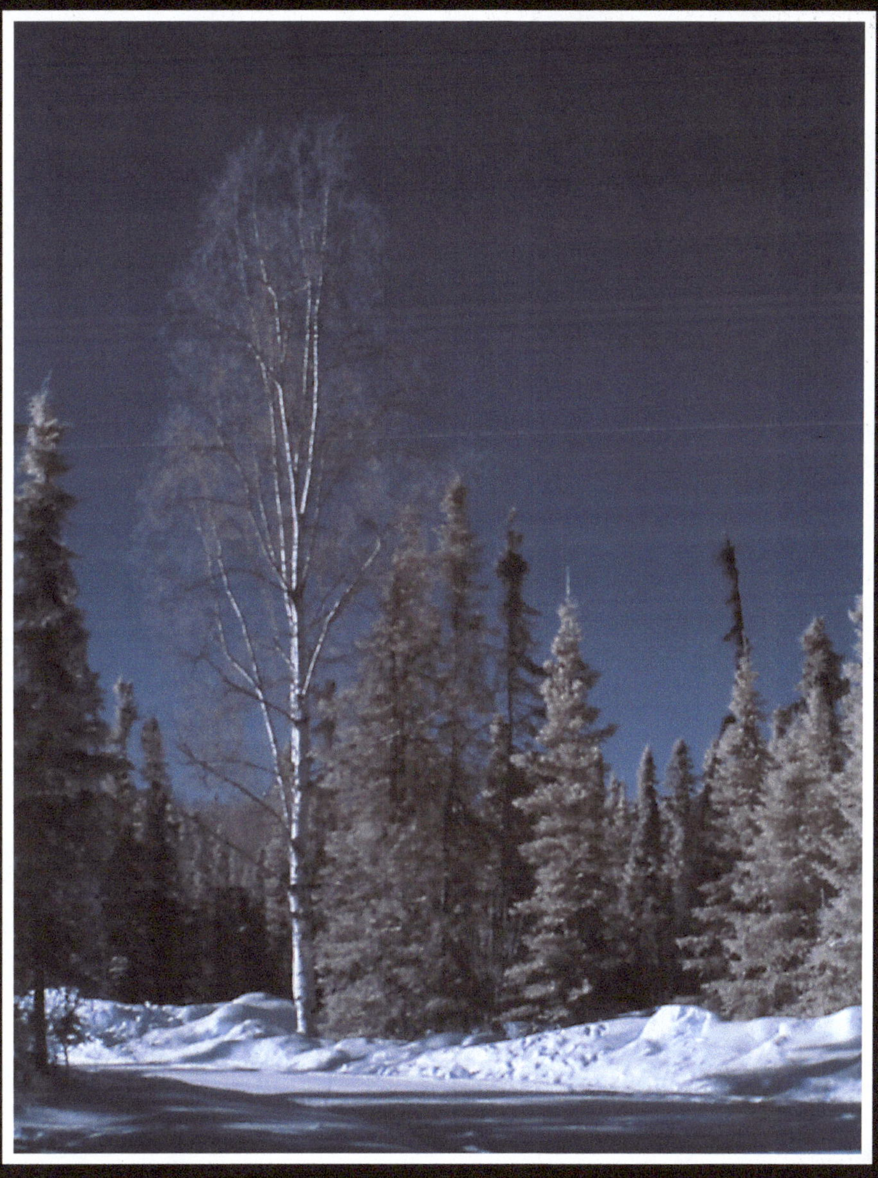

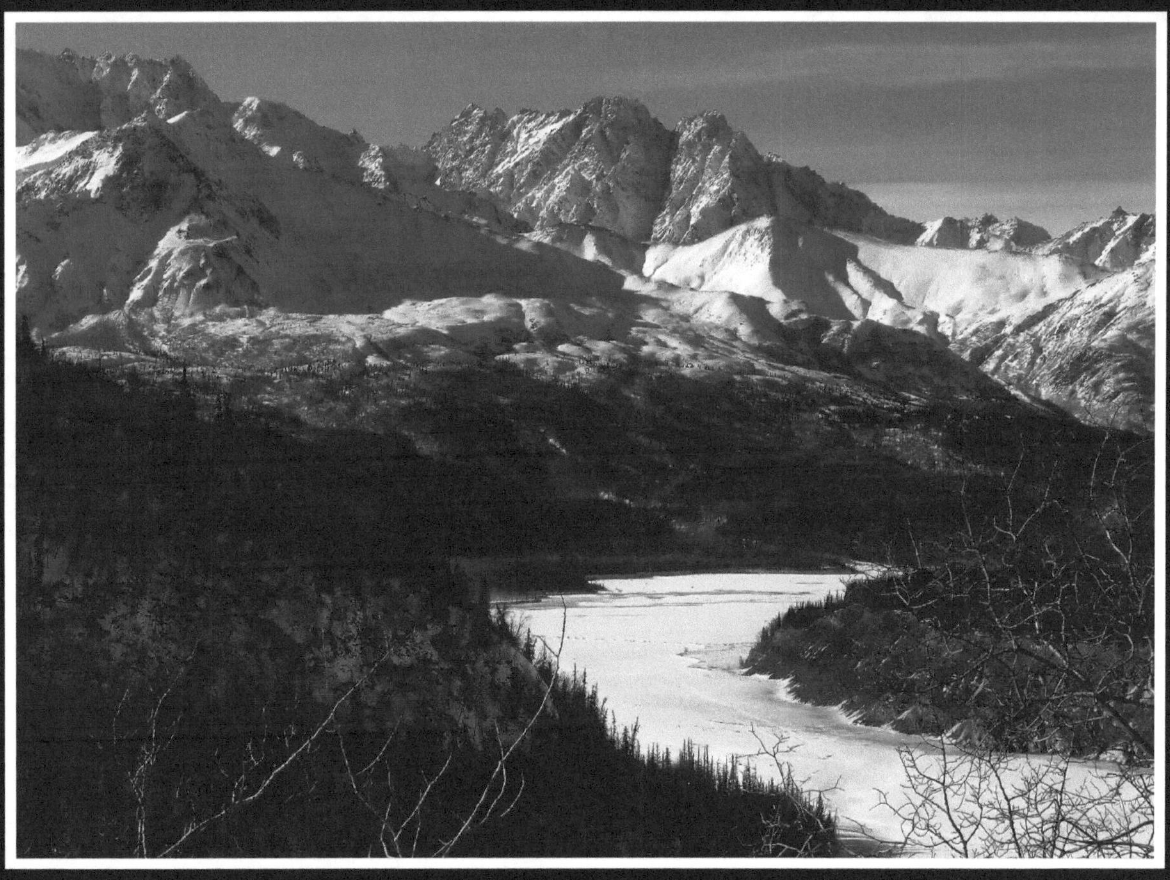

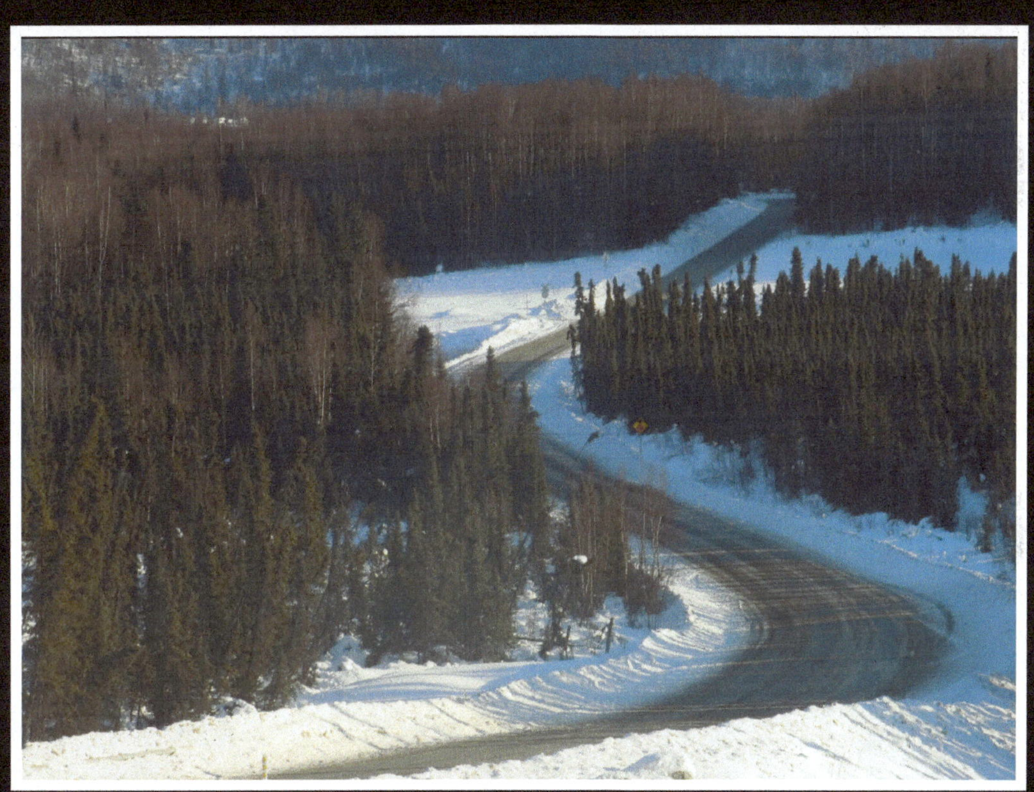

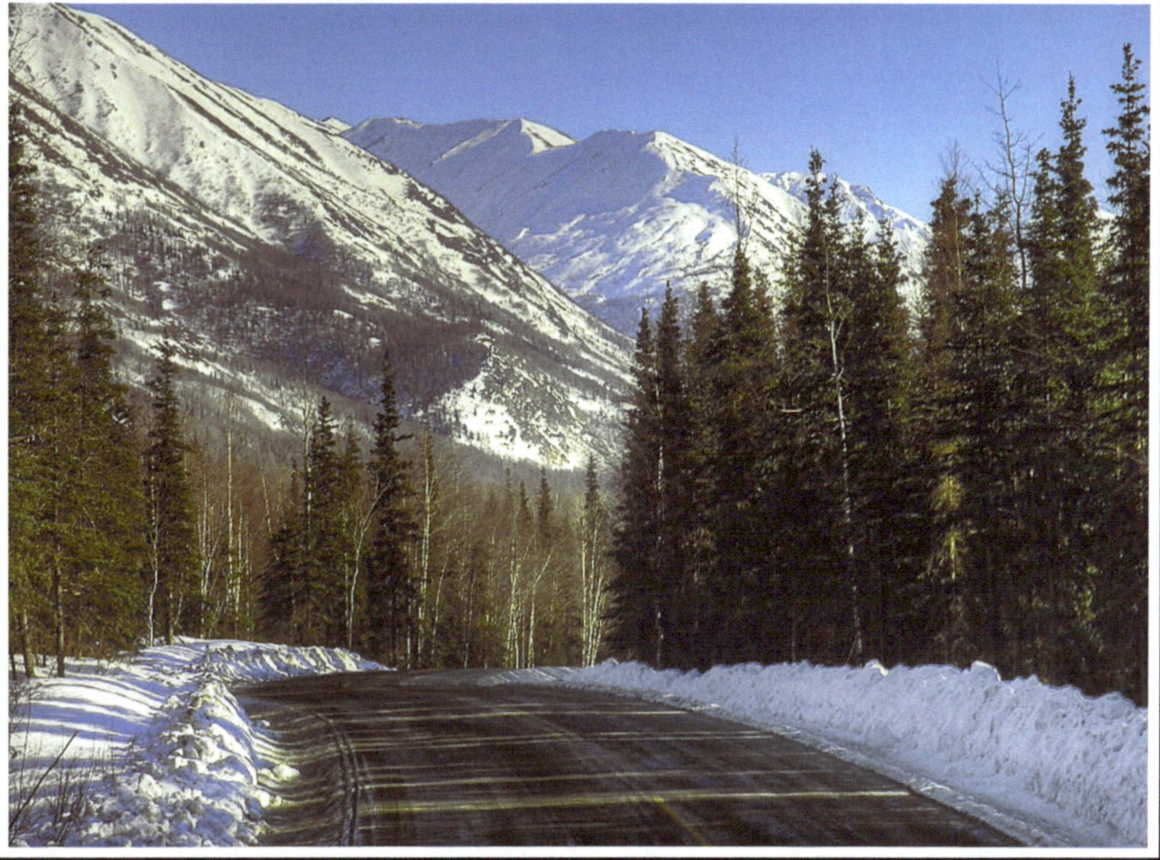

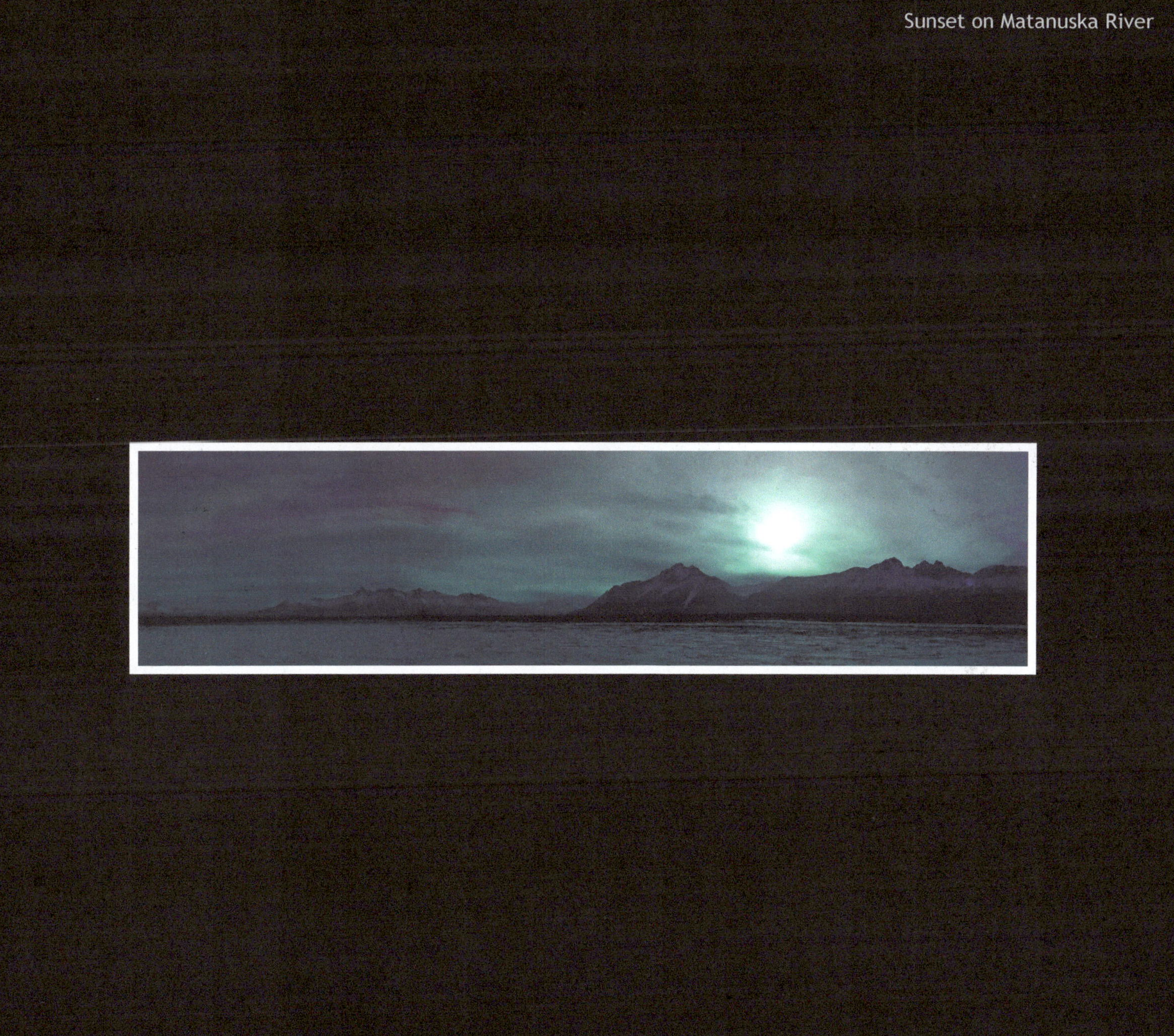
Sunset on Matanuska River

Impressions of Alaska 2007

Earthquake Reminder III

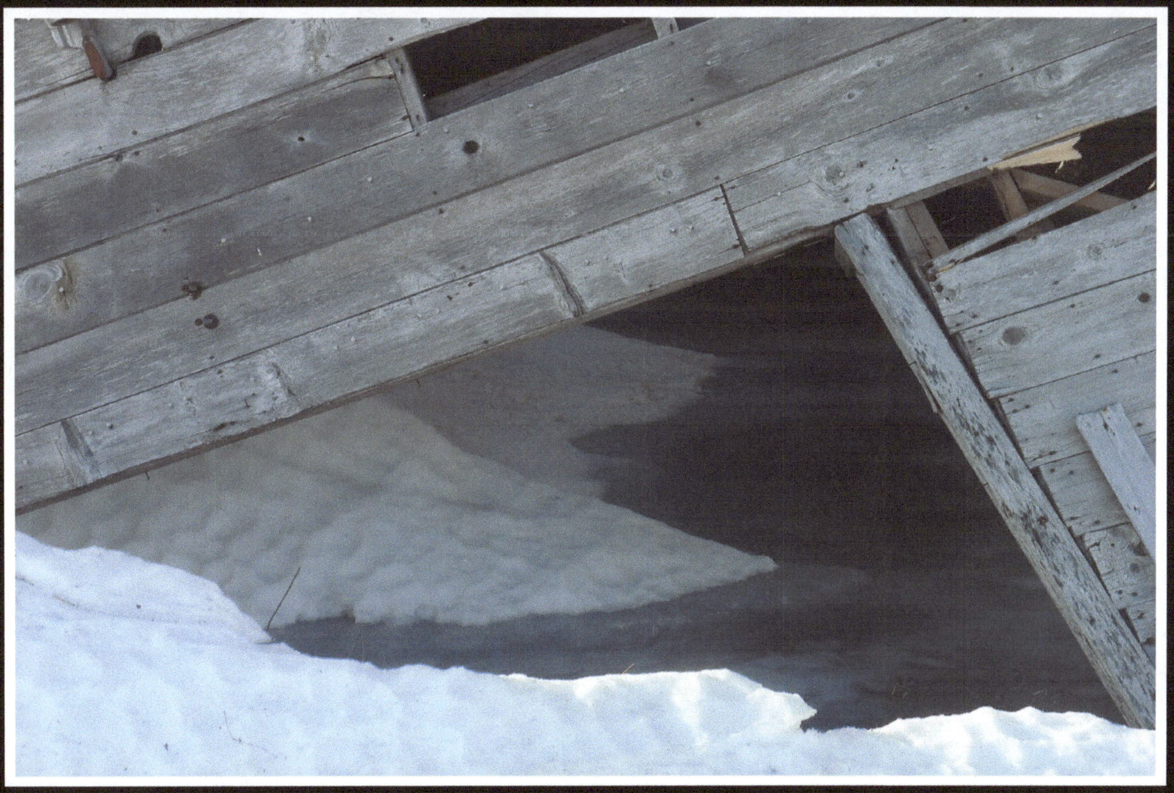

Matanuska River Bend

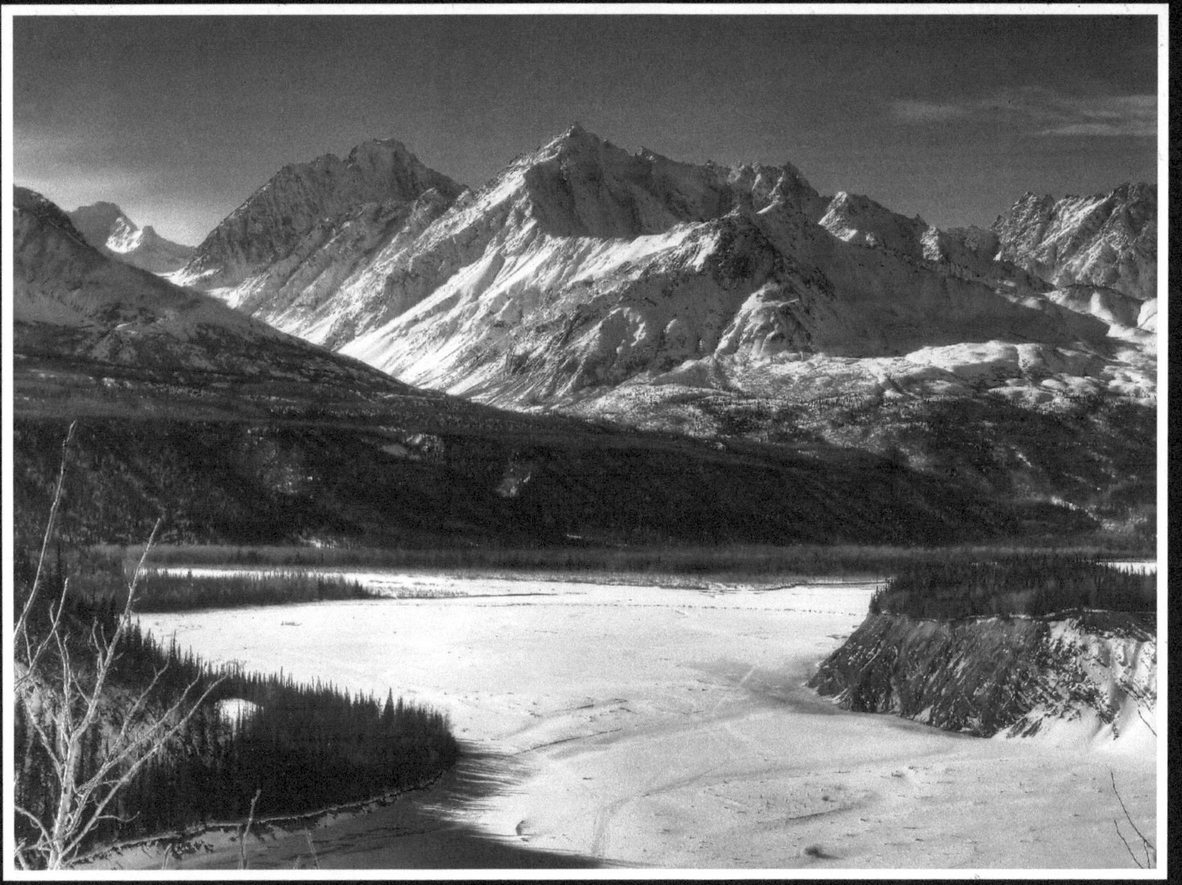

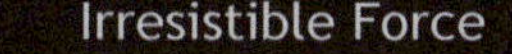

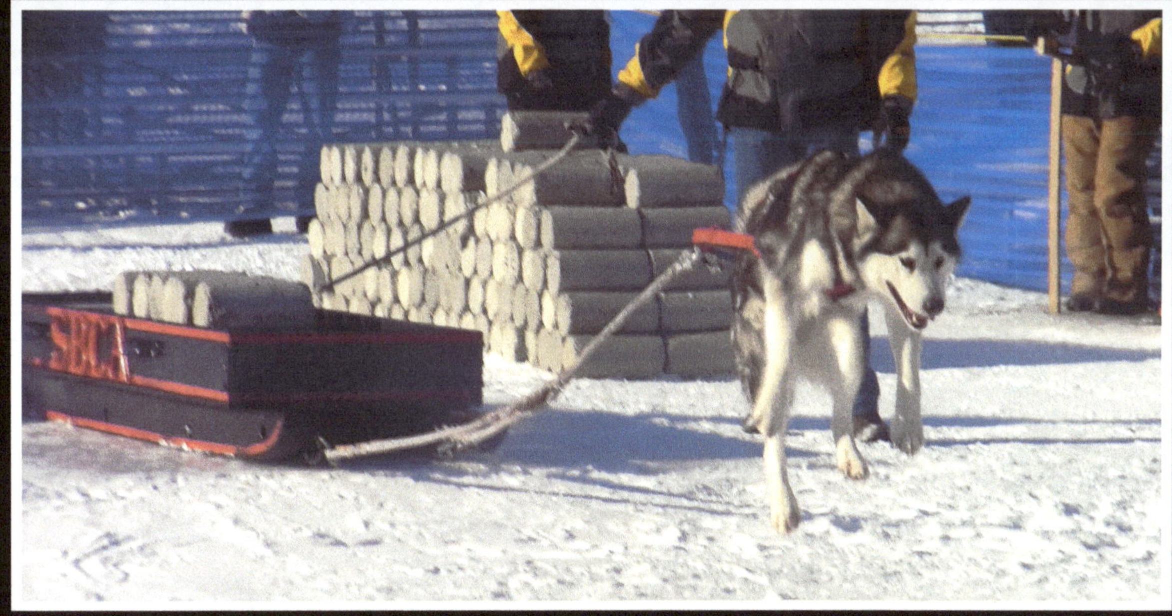
SBCA

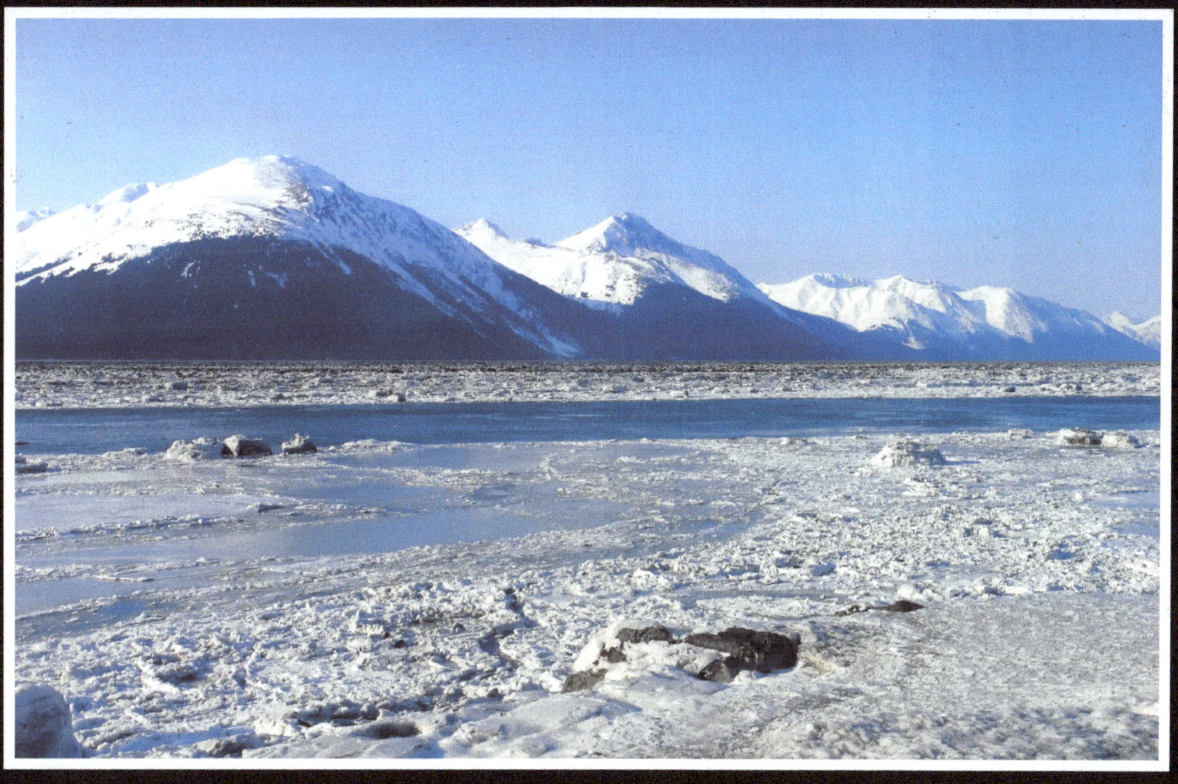

Portage Glacier

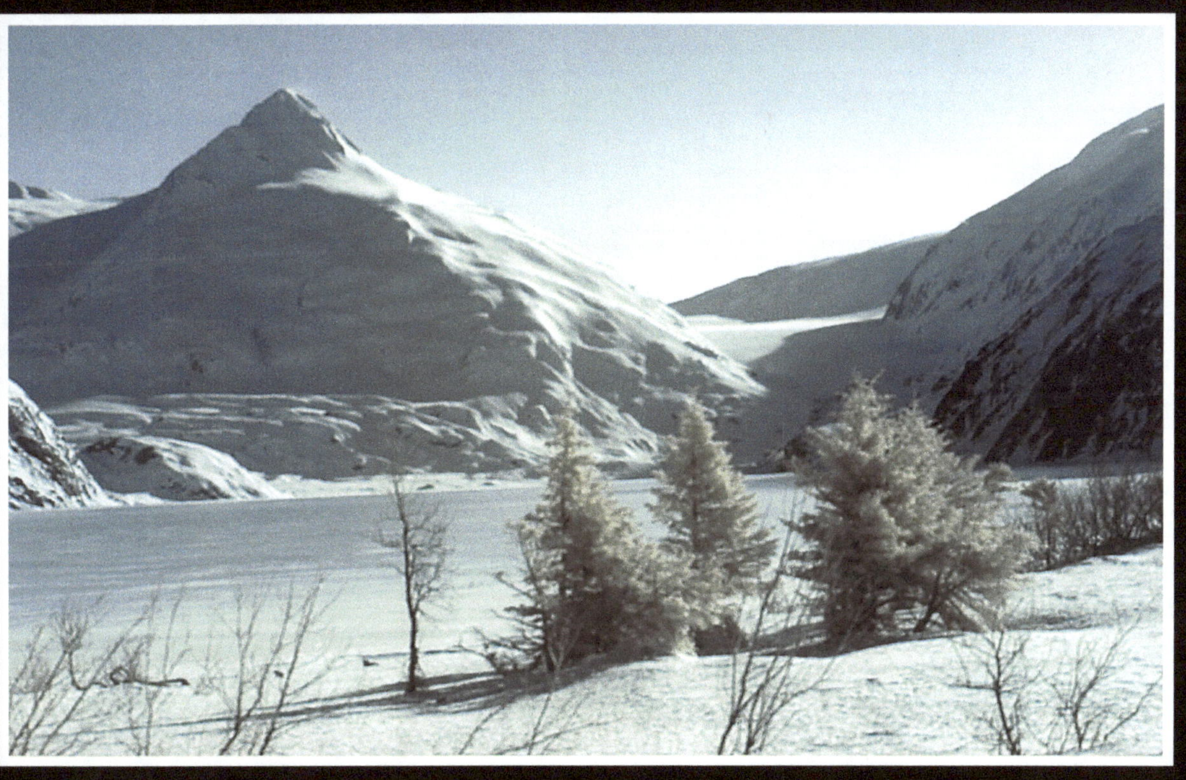

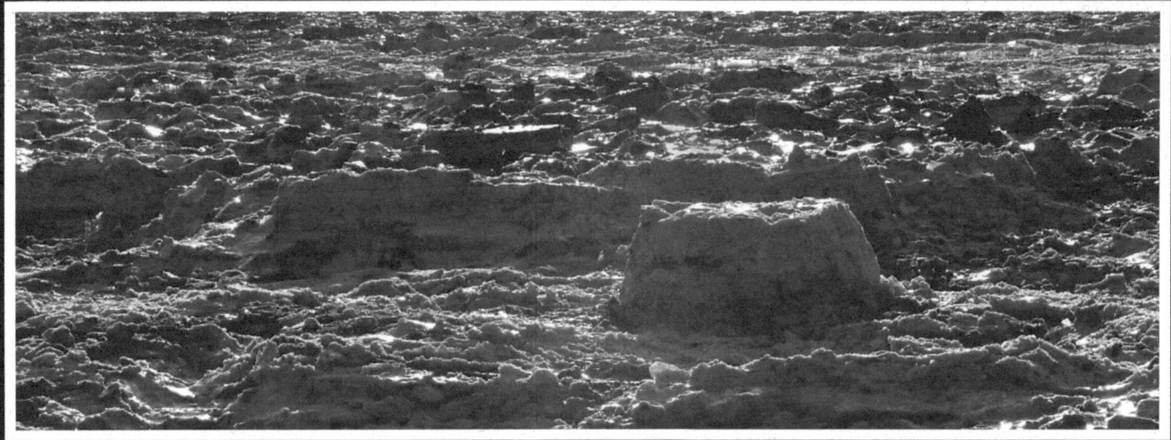

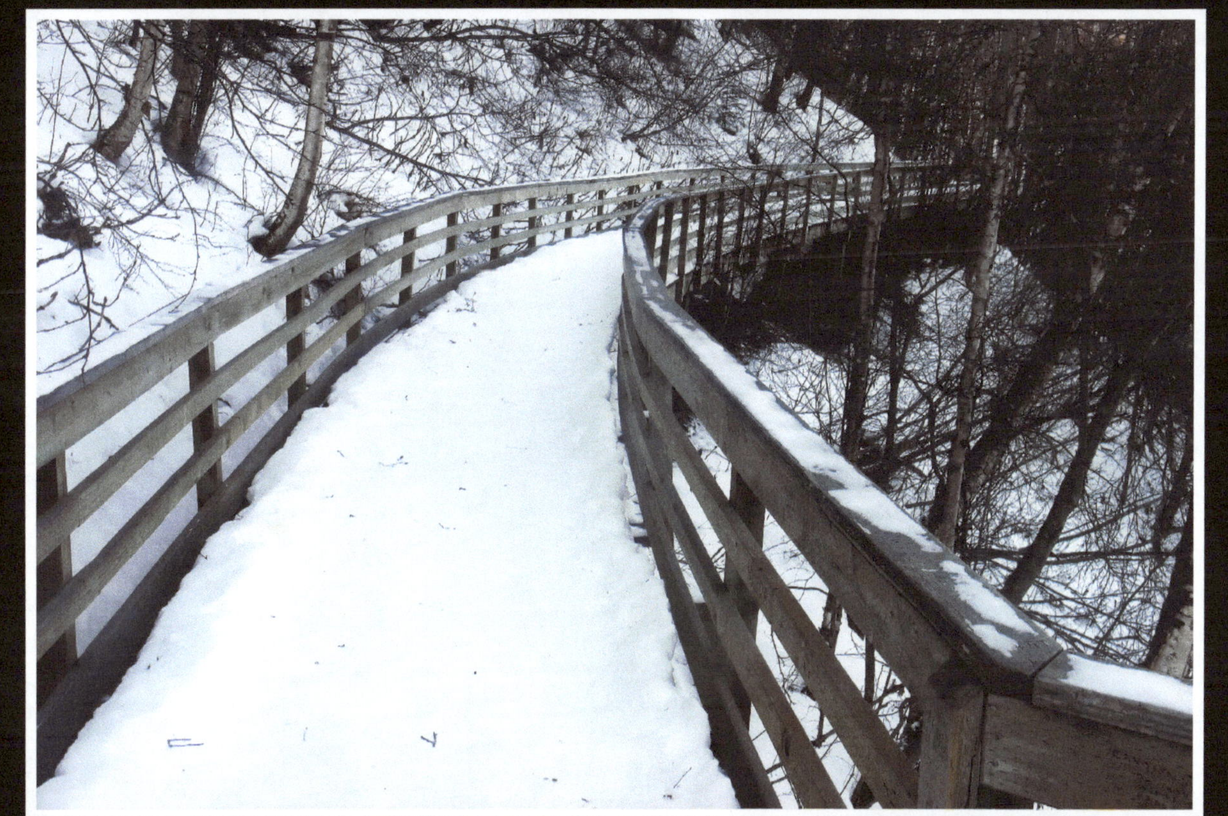

Matanuska River and Mountain II

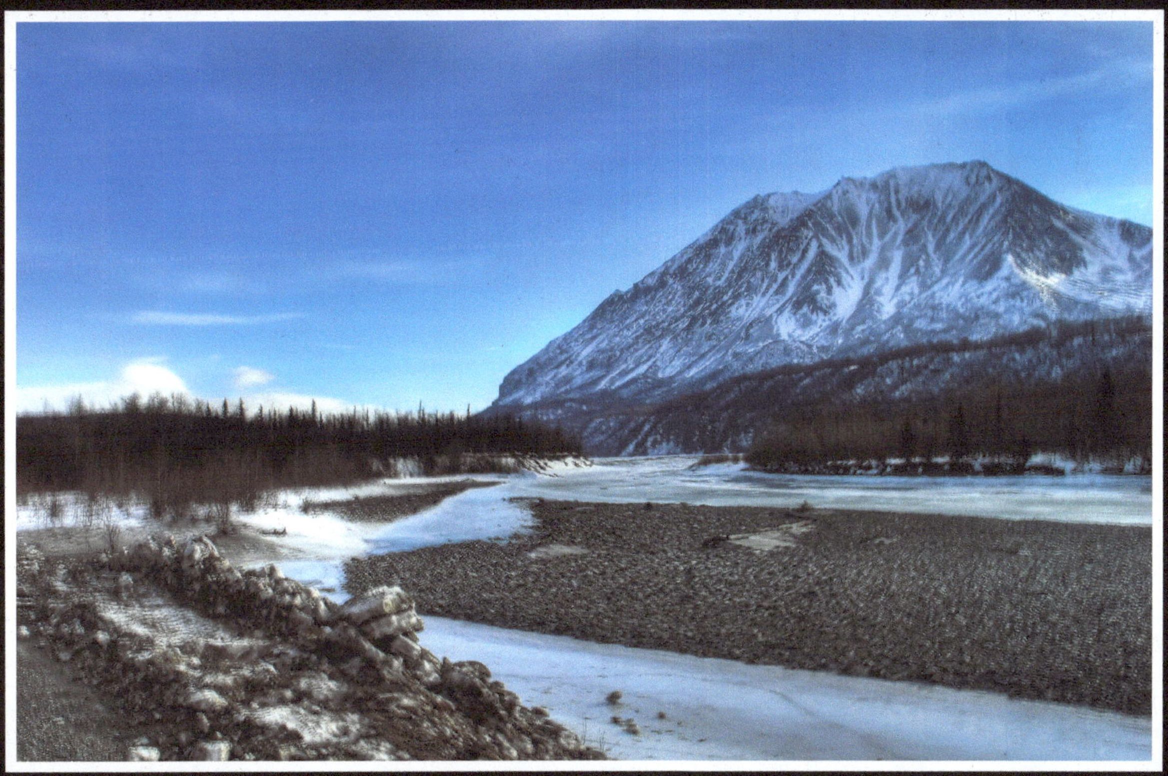

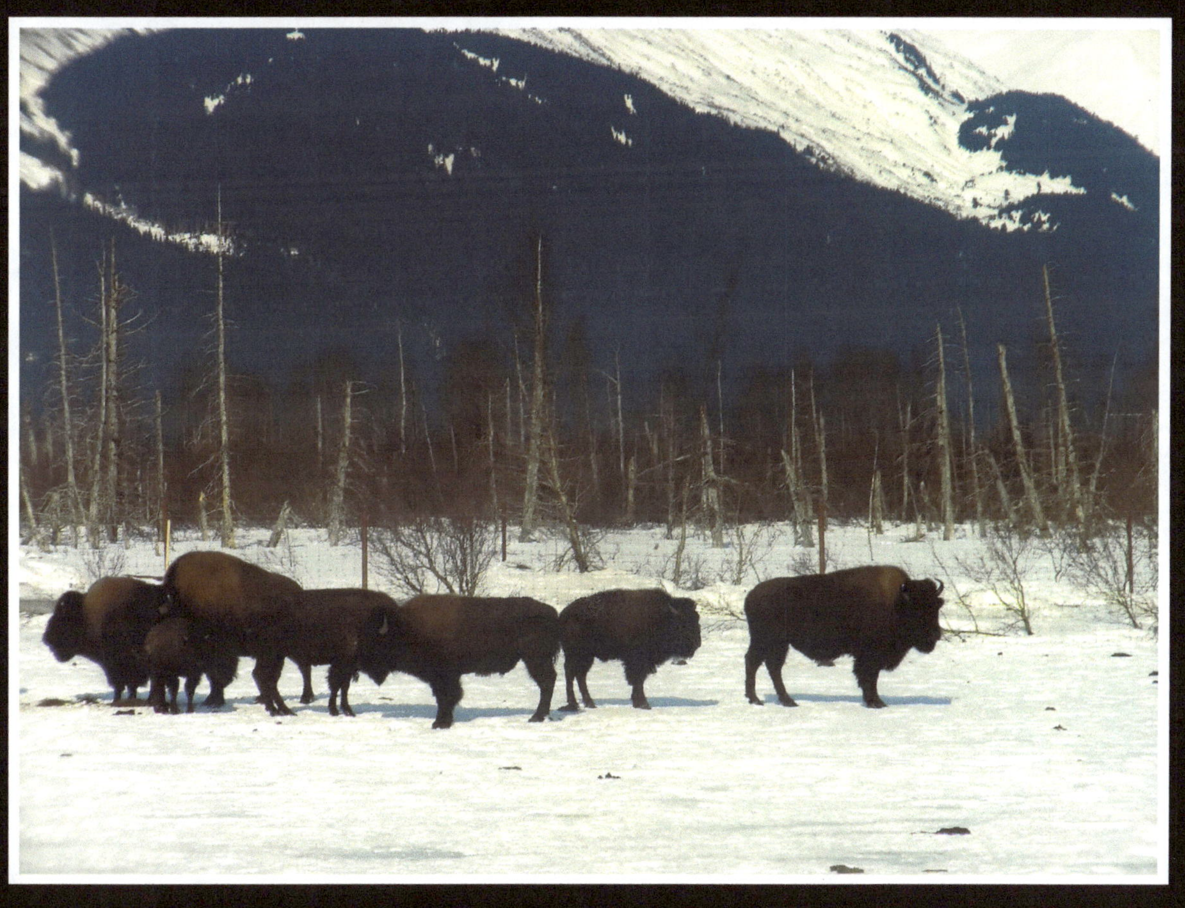

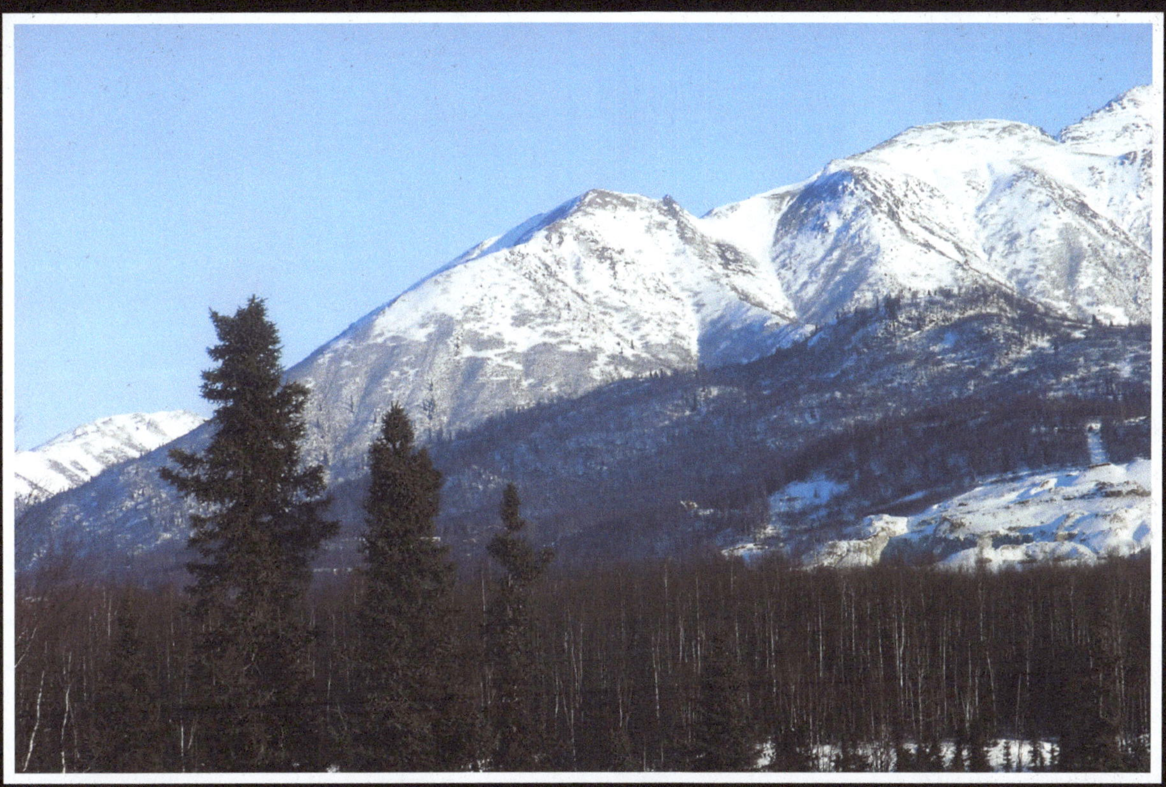

Impressions of Alaska 2007

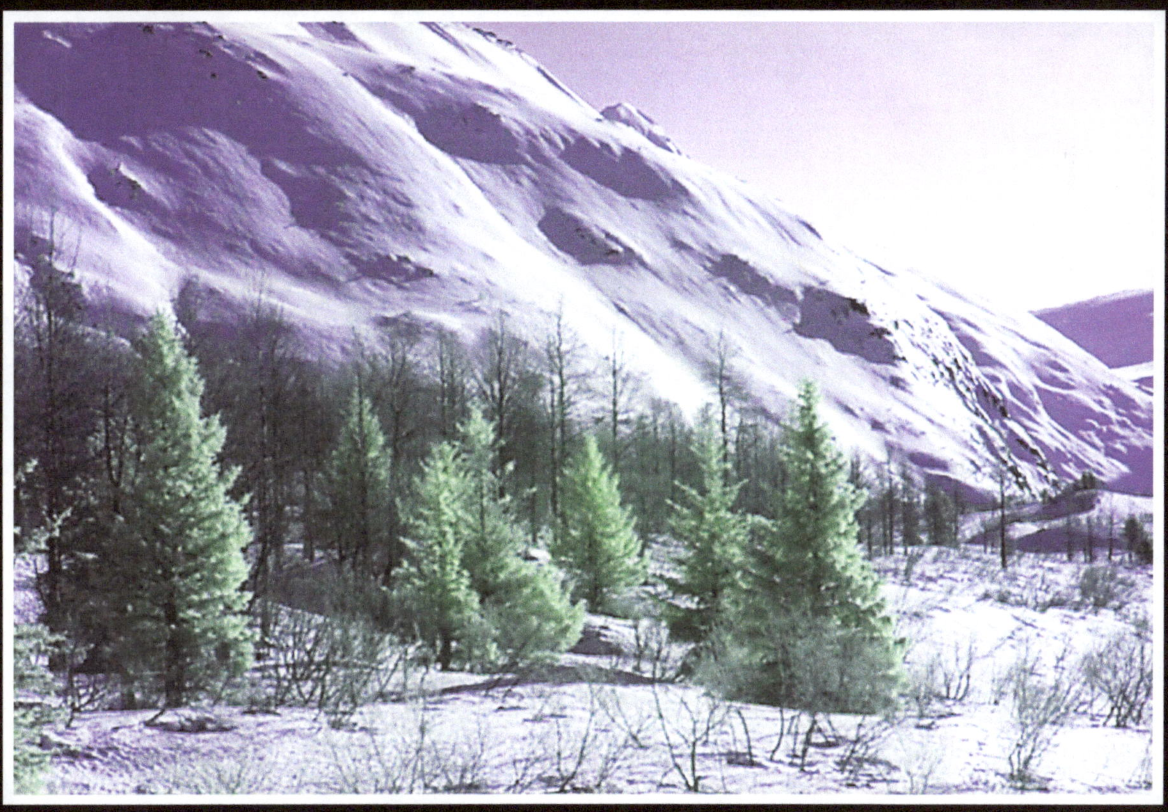

Susitna River near Talkeetna

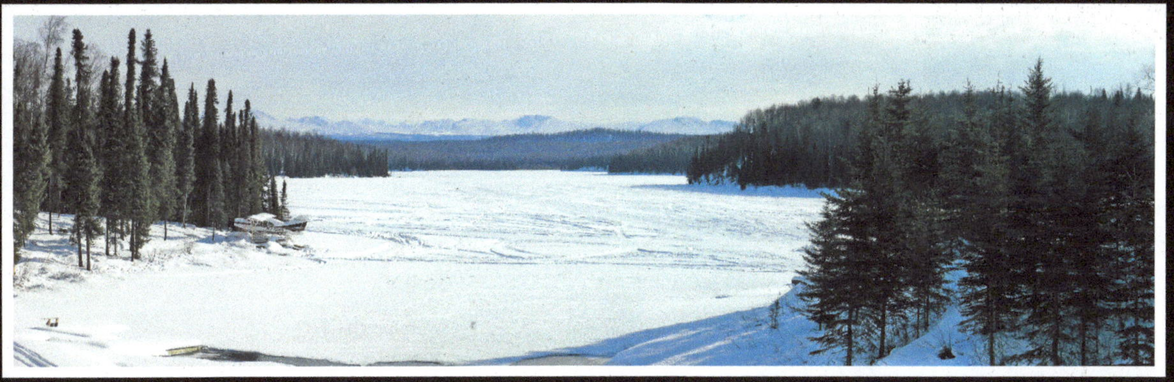

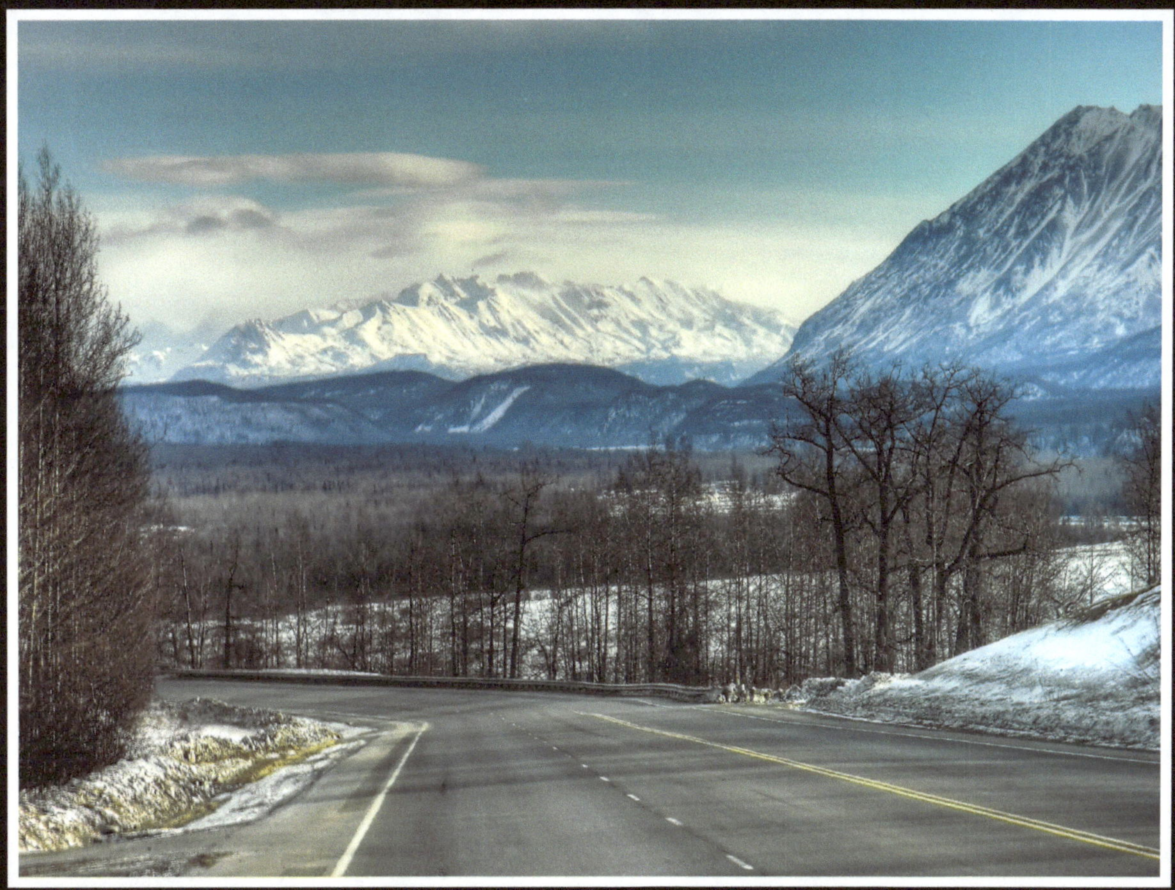

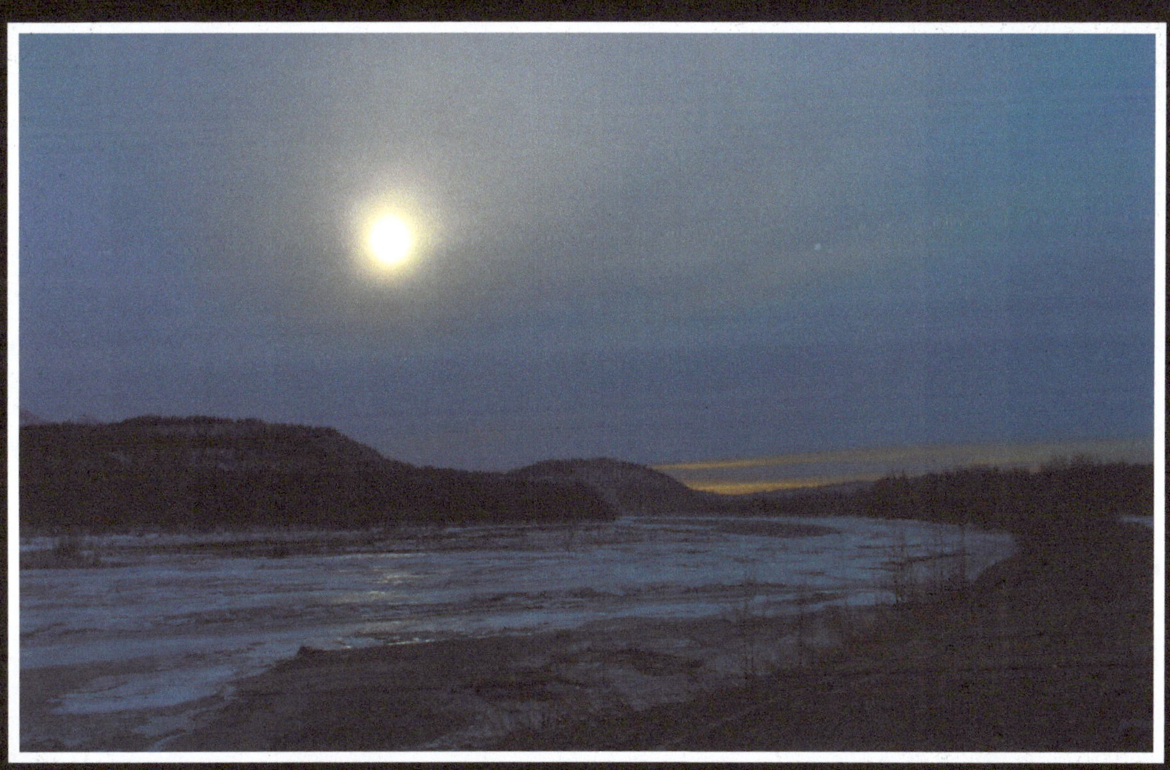

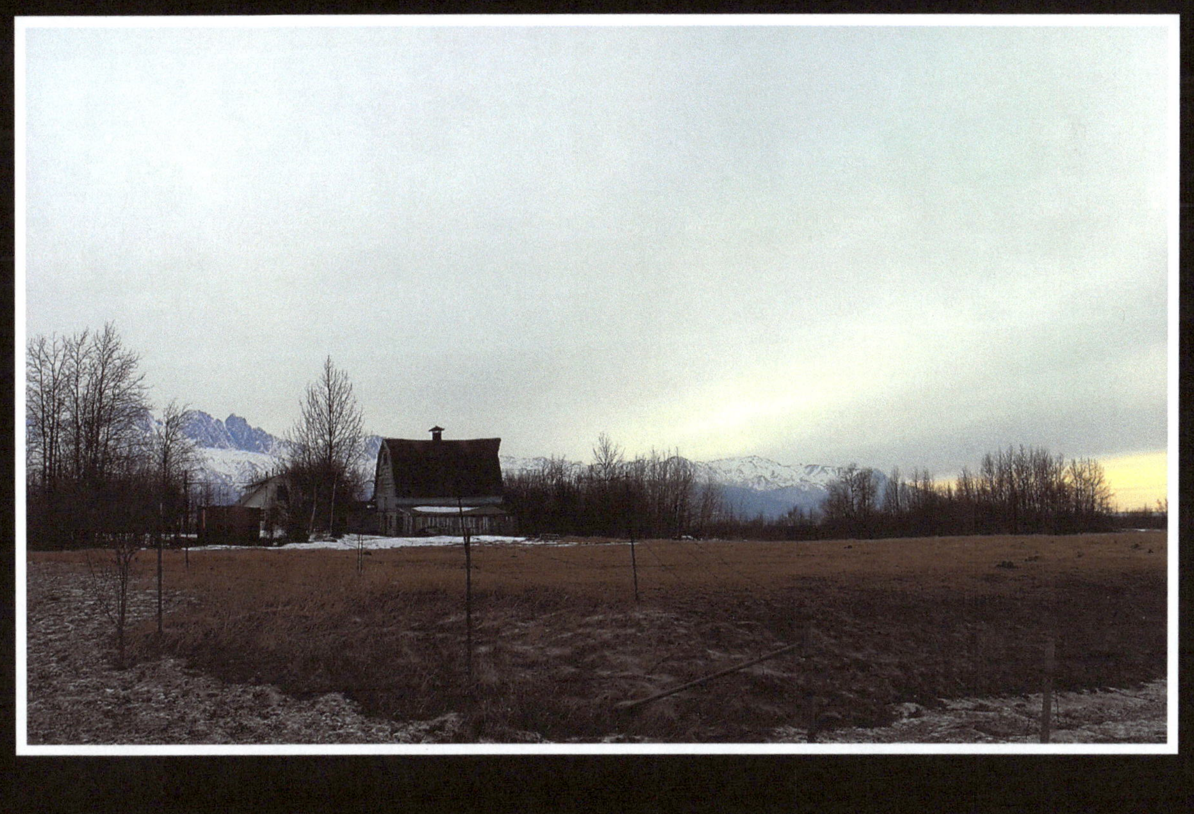

Eklutna Lake

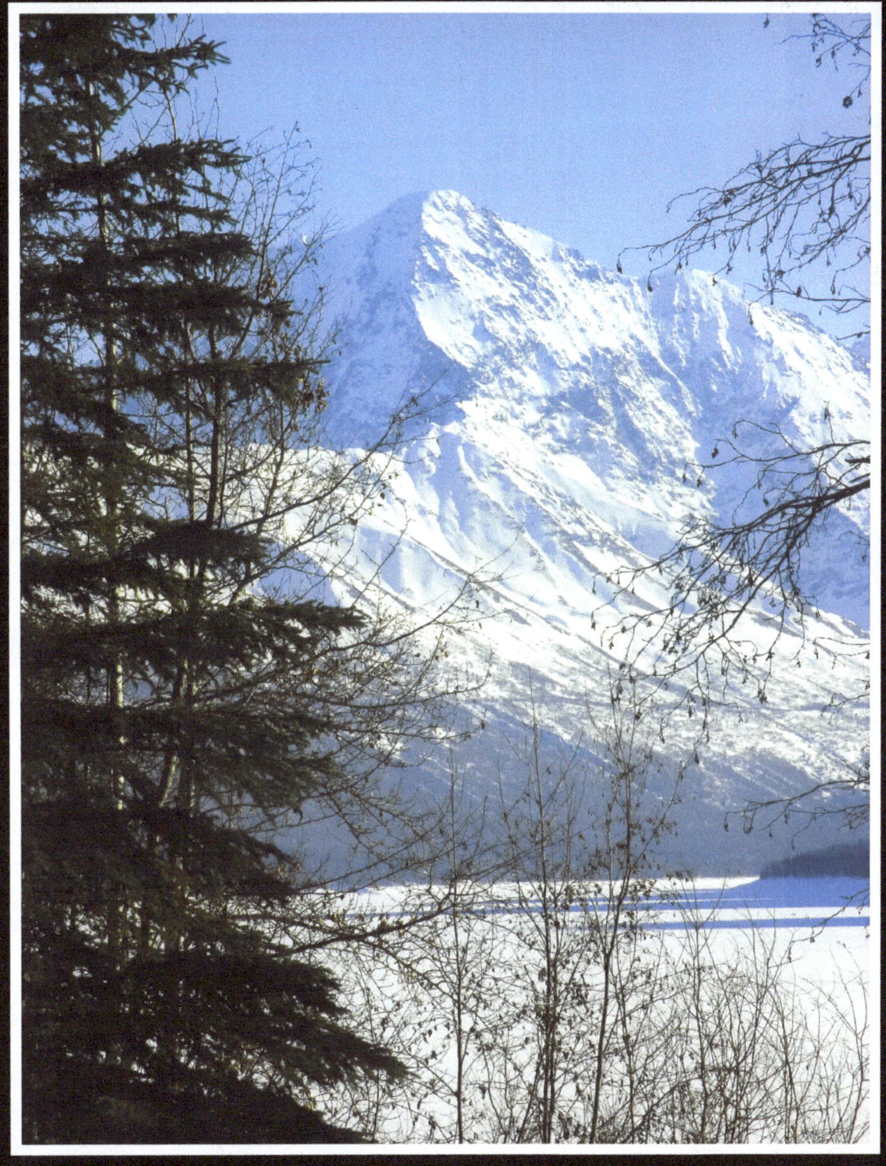

Impressions of Alaska 2007

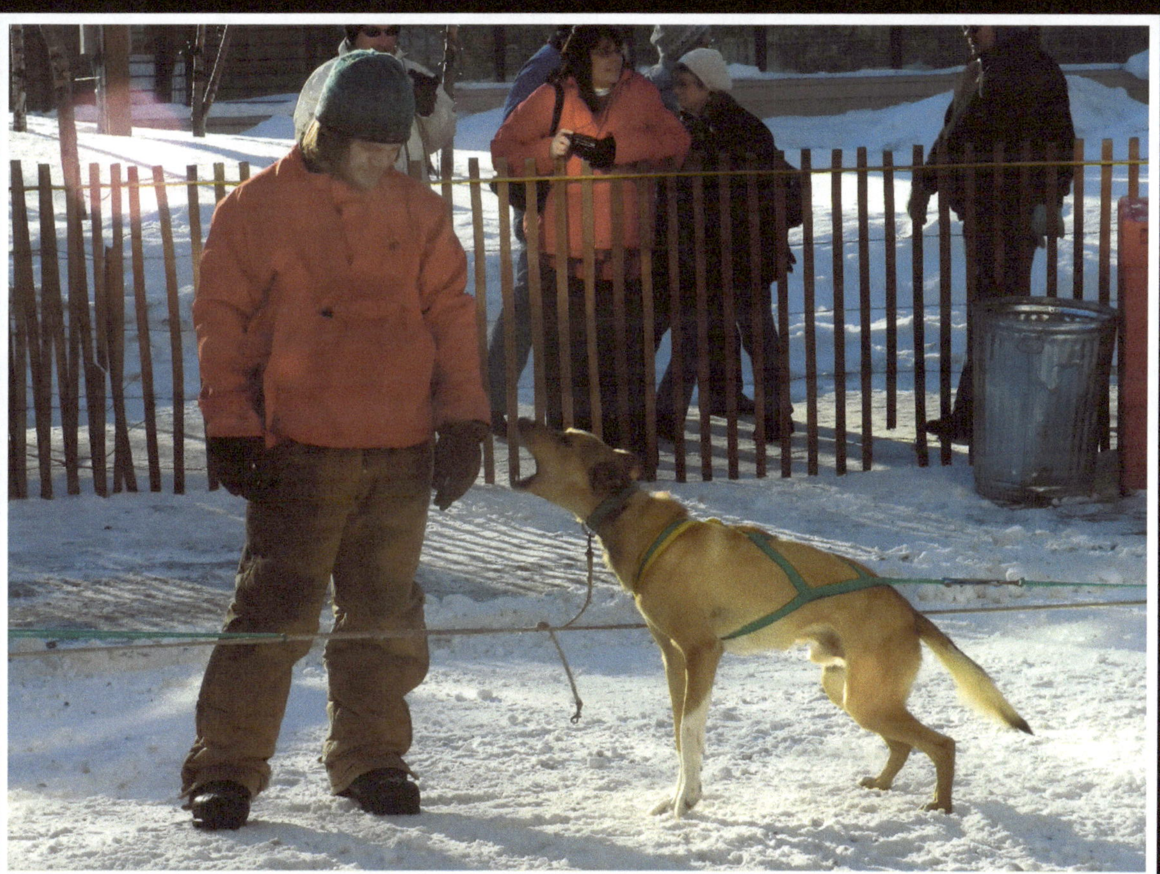

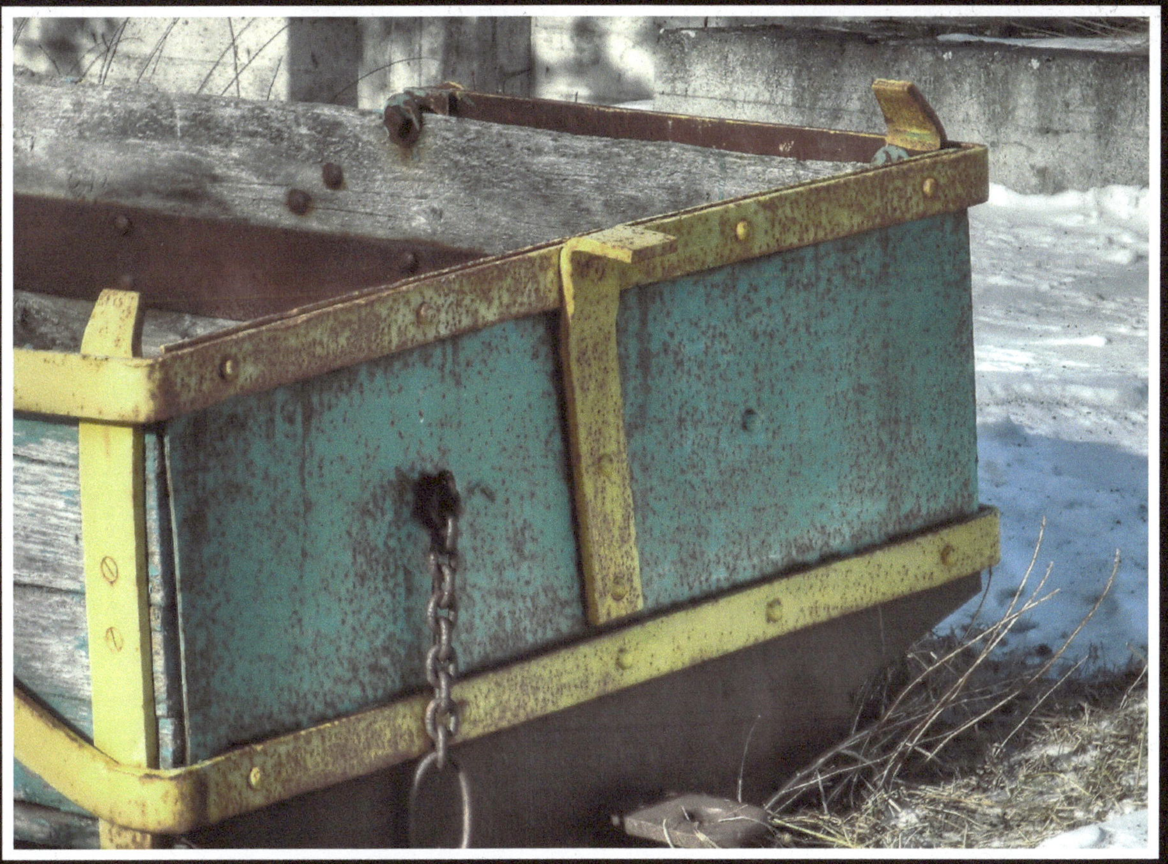

Impressions of Alaska 2007

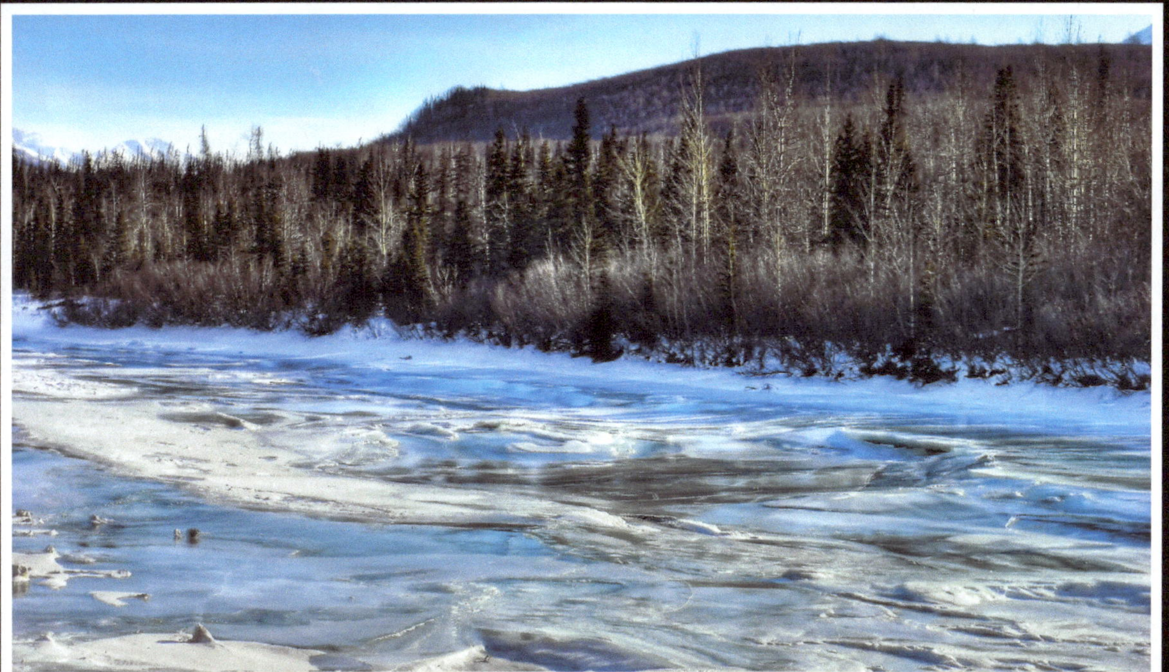

Distant Mount

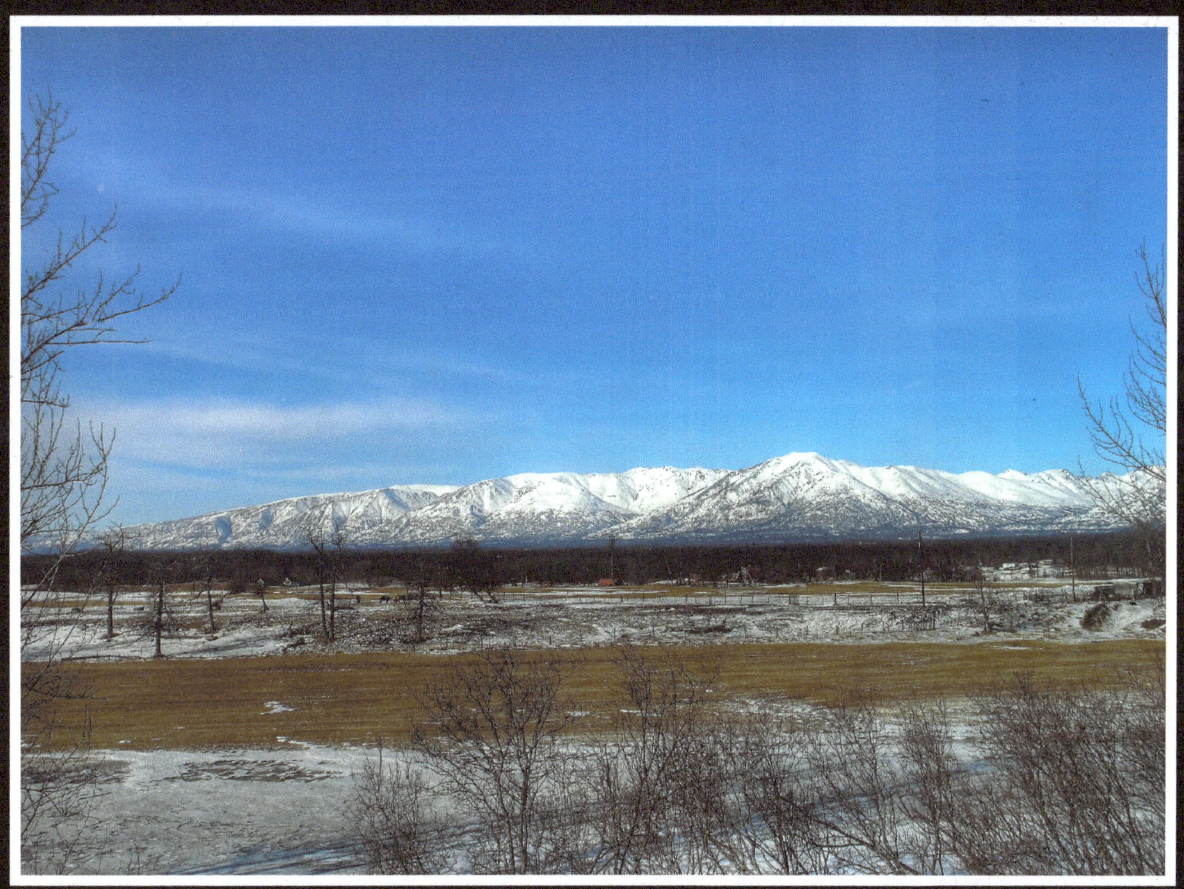

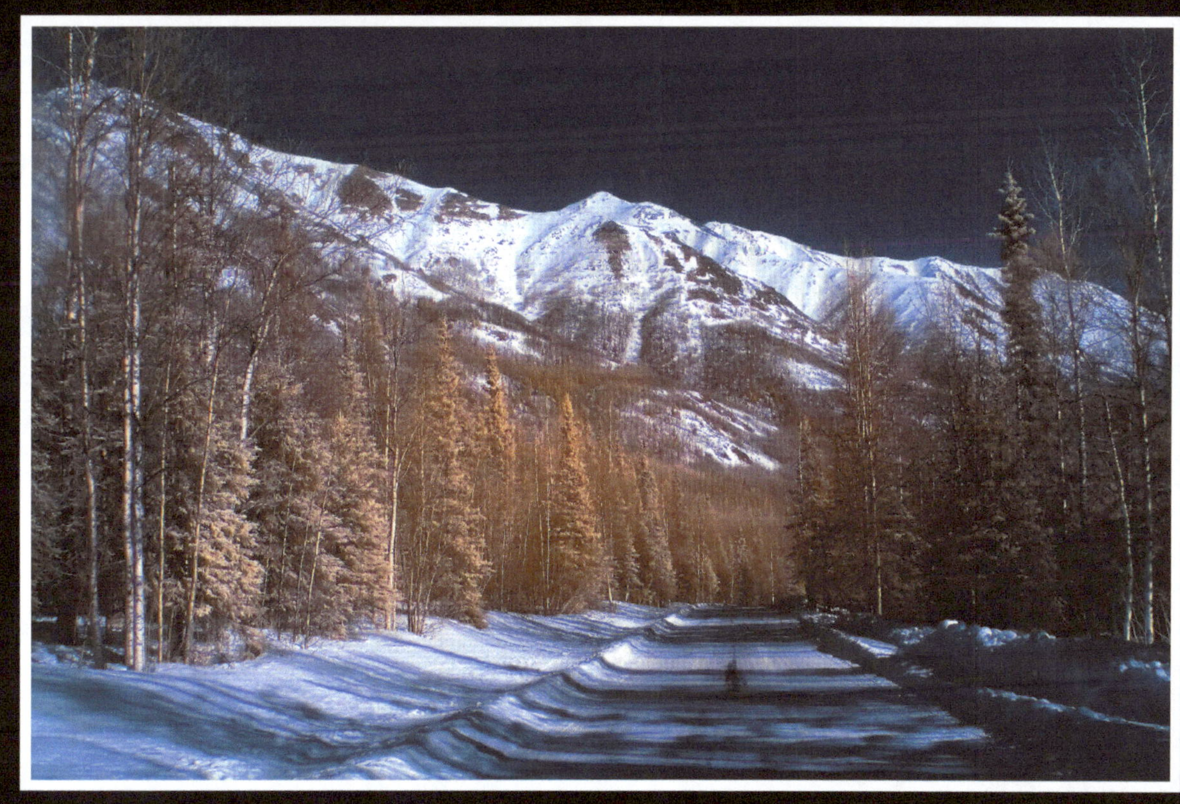

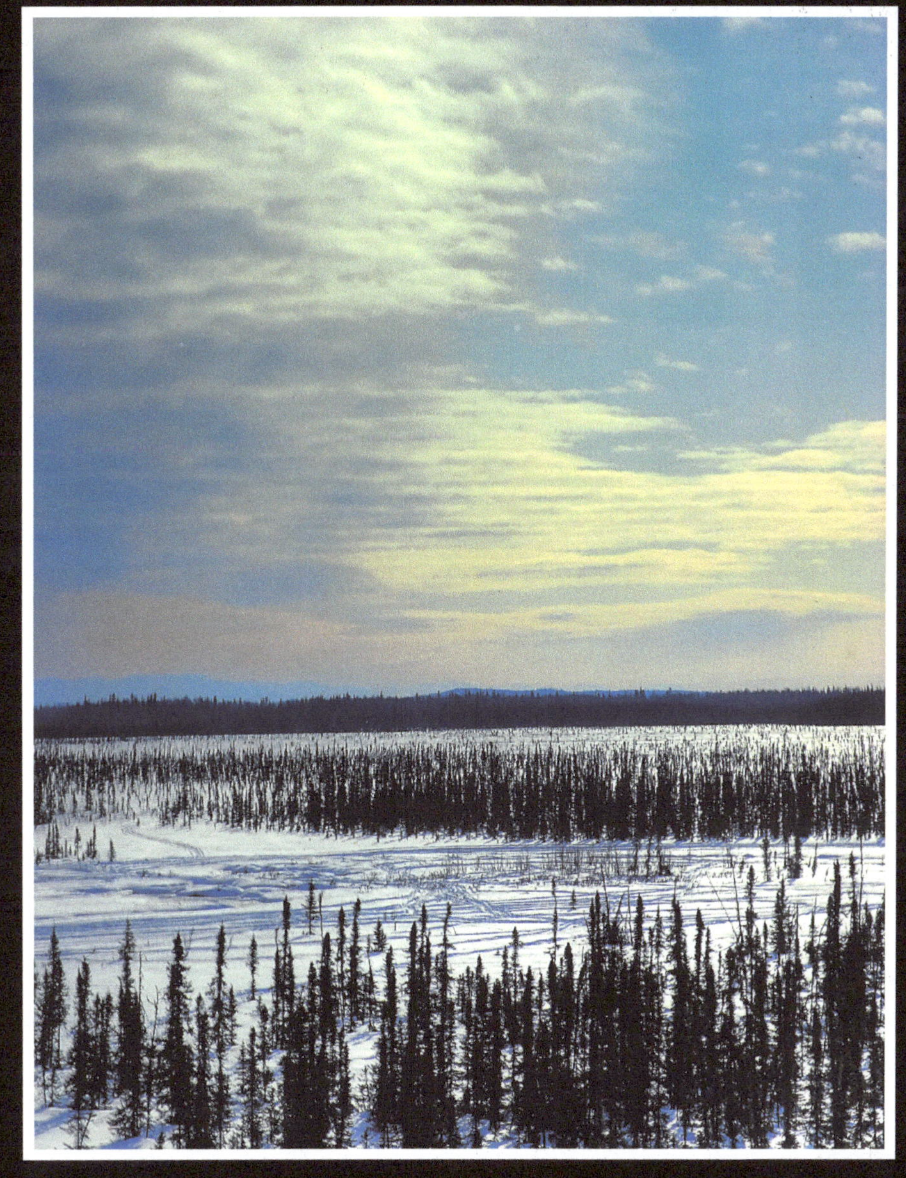

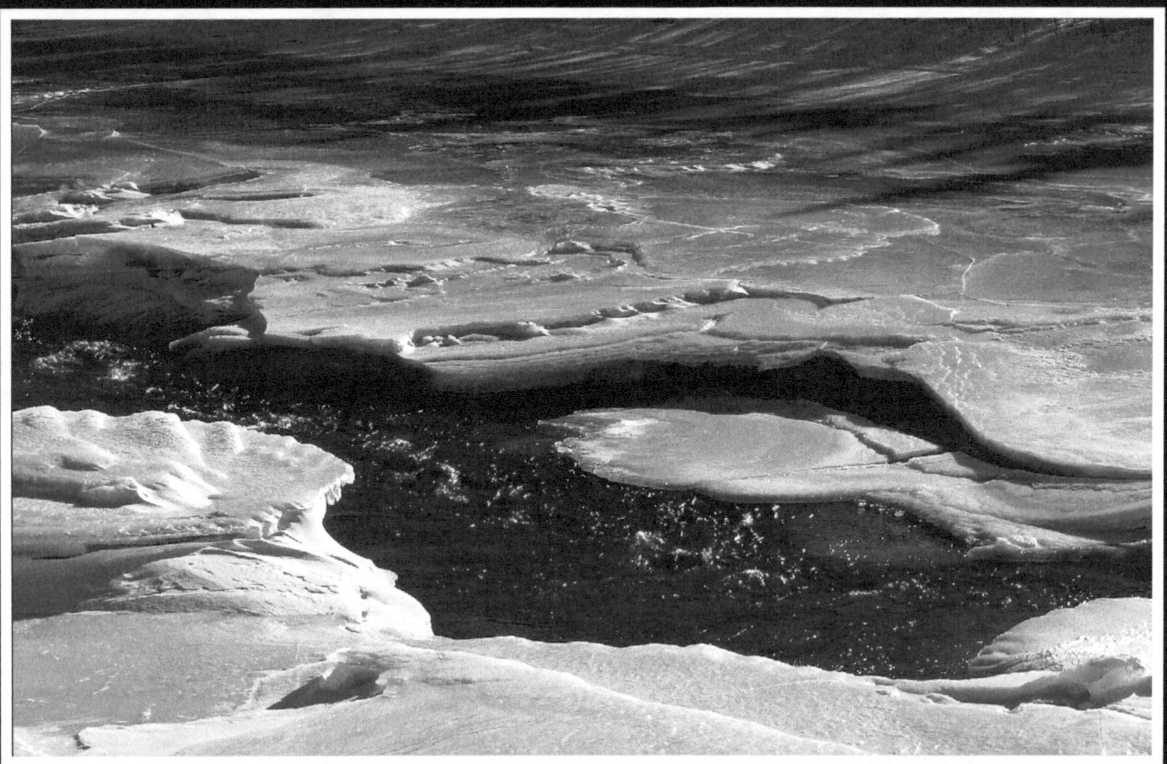

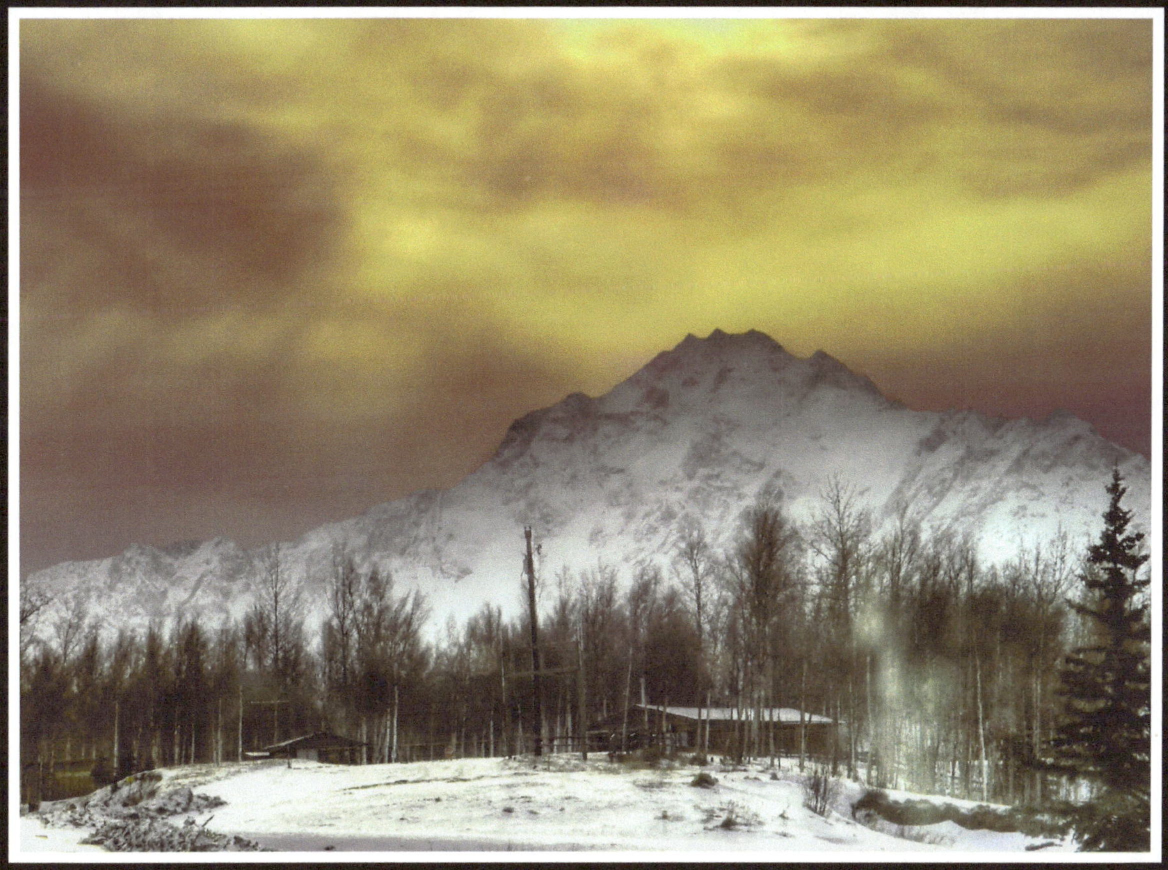

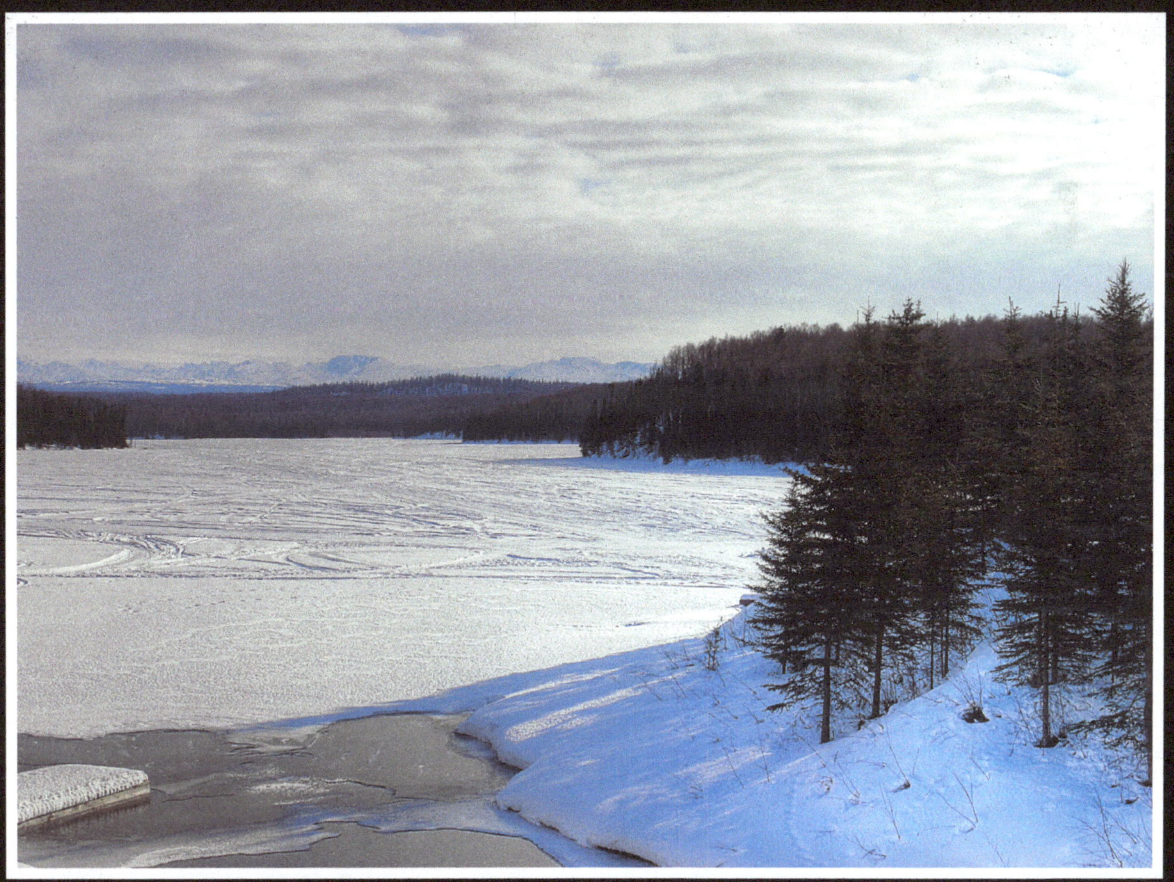

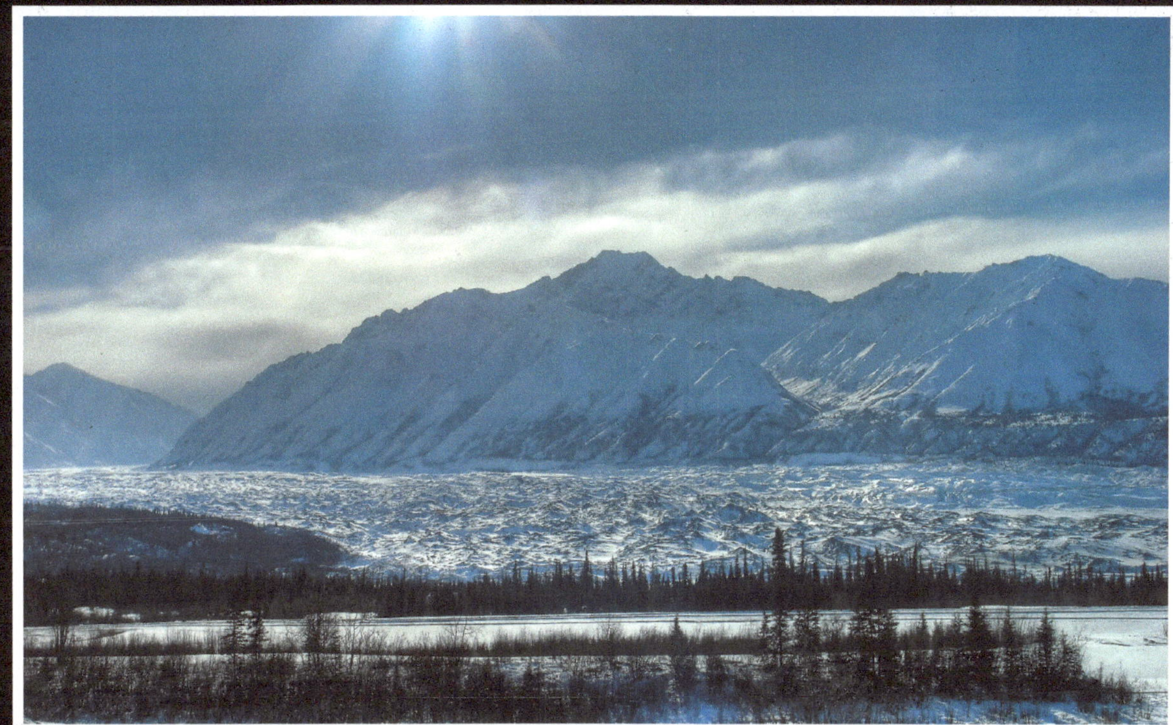

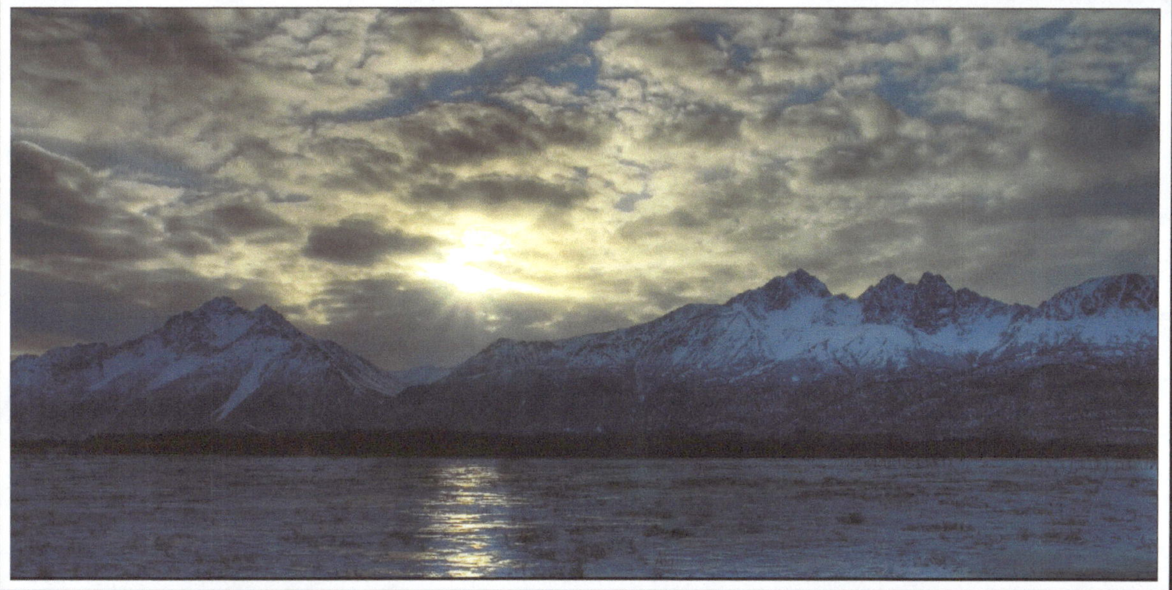

www.ingramcontent.com/pod-product-compliance
Lightning Source LLC
LaVergne TN
LVHW070137110826
845147LV00002B/274

* 9 7 8 0 6 1 5 1 4 5 4 3 3 *